BUDAPEST DIARY

TEXTS AND CONTEXTS : VOLUME 18

BUDAPEST DIARY

In Search of the Motherbook

SUSAN RUBIN SULEIMAN

University of Nebraska Press

Lincoln and London

Fragments from the 1993 Budapest diary appeared in
the electronic journal *Postmodern Culture* 3, no. 3 (May 1993),
Oxford University Press (pmc@unity.ncsu.edu),
and in *Hungarian Quarterly* 34 (winter 1993), 123–33. Copyright
© 1993 by Susan Rubin Suleiman, all rights reserved.
The childhood war memoir in the first chapter appeared in a slightly
different version in *Agni* 33 (spring 1991) and is reprinted
here with permission of the editor. © 1996 by Susan
Rubin Suleiman. All rights reserved. Manufactured
in the United States of America. ⊗ The paper in this book meets
the minimum requirements of American National
Standard for Information Sciences—Permanence of Paper
for Printed Library Materials,
ANSI Z39.48-1984.

Library of Congress Cataloging in Publication Data
Suleiman, Susan Rubin, 1939–
Budapest diary: in search of the Motherbook /
Susan Rubin Suleiman.
p. cm. – (Texts and contexts: v.18) ISBN 0-8032-4256-5
(cloth: alkaline paper)
1. Budapest (Hungary) – Description and travel.
2. Suleiman, Susan Rubin –
Journeys – Hungary – Budapest. I. Title. II. Series.
DB984.4.S85 1997
914.39′120453–dc20 96-774
CIP

SECOND PRINTING: 1999

To those I love—there and here, then and now

CONTENTS

PROLOGUE: FORGETTING BUDAPEST

We were sitting in a cornfield waiting for the sun to set. Mother, Daddy, and I and our guides, a man and a woman who had given us directions from the train station. They knew the border country well and would lead us across once night had fallen.

"You must walk fast, silently," the man told us. "We should reach the village on the other side shortly after midnight. You'll sleep in a house in the village, then first thing in the morning you'll take the bus to Košice."

At nightfall we started our walk. After the cornfields, where the plants grew tall, we had to cross a series of flat, freshly harvested fields entirely covered with stubble. Walking on the stubble was horrible: the sharp ends dug into the thin soles of my shoes and scratched my ankles. I was hanging on to Daddy's hand and gritting my teeth to keep from crying out. Mother walked on his other side.

Suddenly I felt him stumble; he gave a sharp, low cry. "I've twisted my ankle," he whispered to the guide, who had come running at the sound.

"Can you go on? You must go on, there's nothing we can do for you here," the guide said. "Or you can turn back."

"No turning back," my father said. "Just find me a stick I can lean on."

The guide handed him his own thick stick and my father limped along, leaning from time to time on my mother or me. I could see he was in pain, each step an effort. Poor Daddy, he still had a bandage on his stomach from his ulcer operation, and the strain was surely bad for his heart. What would happen to us?

Midnight came and went, and we were still in the fields. The August sky was full of stars, deep and dark and beauti-

3

ful. Gradually I lost track of time and walked as if in a trance. We entered woods, then walked on a road. The sky had faded; it was almost dawn. By the time we arrived in the village, a pale gray light outlined the houses and fences. Every house seemed to have a dog, and every dog seemed to smell our arrival: furious barking accompanied us as we followed our guides down the single street. Finally we reached the house where beds were waiting. "You mustn't sleep long," the guide said. "The dogs have alerted people, you should leave here as quickly as possible." The bus to Košice left at 7:00 A.M.; we would be on it.

An hour of dead sleep, a cup of hot milk, and we were being herded toward the bus. "We're in Slovakia," my mother whispered to me. I had not yet had time to think about that. Now it became obvious, for everyone on the bus spoke a language different from our own. I could see the guide talking to the bus driver, looking at us. The bus driver nodded, smiled, said something. The guide came over: "The bus passes a police station, but it's never stopped. You should have no trouble getting to Košice. Good luck."

And what would we do in Košice? I wondered. How far we still were from America!

The bus rumbled along, only half full at this hour. We sat bleary-eyed among the peasant women taking their wares to market. We had no papers. If by some chance the police stopped the bus, we were done for.

I was beginning to doze off when the bus screeched to a halt. Two men got on, wearing uniforms and carrying guns in holsters. The bus driver accompanied the policemen, talking, as they walked through the bus checking papers. When they stopped in front of us, the driver pulled my mother to his side: "She's my wife," he said in a foreign language—yet we understood him. "All right, but the gentleman and the little girl will have to get off." Next thing I knew, I was following Daddy and one of the policemen into a small building, then into an office with dark wood floors. I knew I was starring in a real-life drama, yet I felt almost nothing. It was as if everything were happening to someone else.

No sooner had we entered the room than the second policeman came running. The two policemen conferred, then I was heading back toward the bus with one of them: my mother had set up such a ruckus, she told me a few minutes later, that they had had to let me go. It was all beyond me: How could they believe she was the driver's wife and also believe I was her daughter if Daddy was my father? Didn't they realize he and I were related? Why had the bus been stopped, when it never was? What would happen to Daddy?

I don't remember our arrival in Košice. We must have gotten off the bus, carrying almost nothing by then, and found our way to a building, a school perhaps, where a large number of Jewish refugees were gathering to leave on a convoy to Israel. My mother spoke to the man in charge. That night we found ourselves sleeping in our clothes on mattresses on the floor of a large room filled with people. They were due to move out in the morning. We didn't know what we would do.

In the middle of the night I was awakened by voices in the room; then a light went on, and I heard a man's voice say "Rubin." My mother sat up. "Here I am," she called. The man in charge approached; he was followed by two other men carrying a stretcher. On the stretcher lay my father.

For a wild moment I thought he was dead. But he was not even asleep; he was smiling at my mother and me.

Later he told us the story. After I had been taken out and he was left alone in the room with the two policemen, they made him sign a piece of paper. He would be taken back over the border, they told him, like all the other Hungarians. This was a popular border crossing; the police were used to returning people. Many simply crossed the border again, they told him with a laugh. They spoke some Hungarian.

After a while my father said to them: "I'm a religious Jew, a rabbi, and I would like to pray. Do you mind?"

"No, go ahead."

He took out his tefilin, the little black leather box and leather straps he put on his arms and forehead every morning, and stood in front of a wall. He put on the tefilin and started to pray, swaying back and forth slightly as he always did. Suddenly, as he prayed, he let himself fall backward and lay stretched out on the floor. The policemen rushed over to him; he appeared to have lost consciousness. After a short while he came to.

"I'm recovering from an operation," he told them. "See, there's still a bandage on my stomach." He opened his shirt to show them the bandage. "I also have a bad heart," he added.

The policemen looked at each other, then at him. He understood they were afraid he might die in the station.

"Is there any way you could send me to my wife and daughter in Košice?" he asked them, still on his back.

That's how he ended up on a stretcher. I have no idea how they found us in the middle of the night. Perhaps he knew about the convoy through the Jewish Community Bureau in Budapest and had told my mother to go there in case of trouble; or perhaps the police took him to the only Jewish place they knew of in Košice. The main thing was that we were together again. Next morning we boarded a train for Bratislava—again without papers. But this time our luck held and no conductor came. In Bratislava we spent a day with my aunt Ica, my father's youngest sister, who had married a Czech doctor. They had both been active in the Resistance and were committed Communists (that would change soon after, when they discovered even the Party had its anti-Semitic streak). My aunt told my father: "Take the first train out of here, no matter where it's going. They're cracking down; you won't make it if you wait."

My father had planned for us to spend the night at his sister's and take the morning train to Vienna. Instead we left that night on a train bound for Trieste. The train was carrying a convoy of Jewish refugees on their way to Israel and was sealed: no stops along the way. My parents did not want to go to Israel. As we neared Vienna, my father fainted again (I assumed it was an act). My mother called for help. The train made an unscheduled stop, and he was carried off on a stretcher, my mother and I accompanying him. After a few days in the hospital he was released. We declared ourselves officially homeless. We were free.

One is the child not only of one's parents. History too nourishes us or deprives us of nourishment. I was born in a Central European capital six weeks before the outbreak of World War II. By the time I turned six, my native city had been invaded by two foreign armies that had fought fierce battles in the streets. By the time I was ten, the Iron Curtain had shut my city off from the other great capitals it had compared itself with. Paris, Vienna, Rome had become off-limits to those who lived in Budapest.

We left Hungary, my parents and I, in the summer of 1949, a month after my tenth birthday. My uncle and grandmother had left the year before, joining my other uncle in America. They had exited with all the proper papers—passports, visas, everything. By the time my parents wanted those papers, they could not obtain them even with bribes; the years of harsh Communism had begun. So they decided to go illegally, leaving everything behind. For me a big adventure was starting again, like the last year of the war—but this time I was older, aware of the loss involved. When we walked out of our apartment on a hot August day, taking a few belongings as if we were leaving on a brief vacation, I told myself I might never again see that house, that street, that city.

For many years I forgot Budapest. I was one of the millions of Americans born in a foreign country, that's all. Budapest belonged to a different life. Then in the fall of my freshman year at Barnard College, young Hungarians began arriving in New York, refugees from the 1956 uprising; I became involved in relief efforts organized on campus. Speaking Hungarian again with people my age rather than with my parents or my aunts and uncles thrilled me. Were these my true compatriots, these young men with restless eyes who spoke no English and looked bewildered? For a few days I thought I was in love with a high-cheekboned, blue-eyed boy who assured me that deep breathing next to an open window every morning, even in the coldest weather, had given him the spiritual strength to fight the Russian tanks; after that he had hopped on a truck racing for the border. I tried deep breathing a few times, standing by my open dormitory window overlooking the traffic on Broadway. But the December chill made me shiver, and besides, my freedom fighter left New York to attend college in the Midwest. By Christmas break I had lost interest in both yoga and Hungarians.

Very few people notice I have a slight accent when I speak English, and to my own ears I sound like any other East Coaster. Had I been only a year or two older when I arrived in this country, I would now speak English with a rolling *r* and deep vowels, and that insistent monotone I recognize anywhere, even in the noisiest restaurant or crowded elevator. Instead, American speech, singsong, became my home. Although I never forgot my native tongue, my knowledge of it was frozen in time: my vocabulary and syntax remained those of a fourth-grader. As I progressed through college and graduate school, I acquired great funds of knowledge about French and English and Italian history and literature, but my ignorance of Hungarian history and literature continued undisturbed. Later I made sure both of my sons learned French, since their father and I often spent long periods of research and writing in Paris, but it never occurred to me to teach them any Hungarian words or tell them about their Hungarian heritage. My husband, an Iraqi Jew, felt the same way about Arabic, which he spoke with his parents: our children grew up ignorant of both our native tongues. Perhaps not unrelated to that, both tongues had a complicated history for Jews.

The very words "national heritage" seemed to me fraught with ambivalence, as they must be for any European Jew. Were the picturesque horsemen of the Hungarian plains, not far from my mother's birthplace, part of my or my children's heritage? Then what about the "Jewish laws" of the 1920s and 1930s, which barred access to university education for all but a few Jews, or the murder of thousands on the streets of Budapest by Hungarian Nazis in the fall and winter of 1944? Were they part of our heritage too? I didn't tell my sons about my memories from the last year of the war or about the adventure of escaping from Hungary on foot. It was as if my past had never existed.

Everything changed when my mother fell ill. It was the fall of 1983, and she flew to Boston to consult a specialist. By then I was separated from my husband, a single mother trying to earn tenure as a Harvard professor. There was little time in my life for chitchat, especially with my mother: for many years we had observed a friendly truce after the battles of my adolescence, but part of the agreement was that we would never—almost never—speak about the past. Not about Budapest, not about our escape or our arrival in America, not about my father's premature death. After many years of widowhood, my mother had remarried. Her devoted new husband, a mild-mannered Hungarian dentist who had retired to Miami after his first wife died, relieved me and my sister (born after we left Hungary) of the obligation to call her often. When I did call, we spoke about trivia. If my mother avoided the past, I avoided the present: I couldn't tolerate her concern for me, which I knew was genuine but which I experienced as an invasion. I didn't want her sympathy.

When she arrived at the house, I was struck by the change in her. Six months earlier, at my son Michael's bar mitzvah, she had worn a purple dress that made her blue eyes sparkle; no one would have guessed she was almost seventy-five years old. Now she looked shrunken. She had recently been diagnosed with temporal arteritis, an old-age disease for which the only effective medication was cortisone; but the drug was killing her, psychologically if not physically. Her fine, beautiful face had become coarse and bloated, her hair had started falling out; soon her skin would become so thin that the slightest bruise would bleed and create ugly scabs over her arms and legs. She had always been proud of her good looks; she regarded these changes in her body not as a disease to be coped with, but as a death sentence.

The only thing that still cheered her up (later, even that would go) was being with her grandchildren. On that visit in particular, they had a grand time. My older son, in an elated mood, got her to teach him some dirty words in Hungarian, and he and his brother went around the house singing them with glee, mispronouncing all the words. "Csirkeszar, csirkeszar, edd meg csirkeszar." "Chicken shit, chicken shit, go eat chicken shit." My mother, a thing rare for her now, laughed and laughed.

Watching her play Rummikub with the boys one night (she loved the game; it was a version of the gin rummy she and my father had played with friends during summer evenings in Hungary), I suddenly *saw*, as clearly as if projected on a screen, my mother as a young woman, holding my hand as we walked down a boulevard in winter, setting our faces against the wind and playing the multiplication game. What's eight times seven, what's seven times four, what's three times nine? The questions came faster and faster, until we were both tripping over our tongues and laughing. How I had loved her, my beautiful mother who knew how to play!

I decided before the end of my mother's visit that I had to take my children to the place where I had known that young woman. I told myself I expected no great revelations from Budapest; but I desired to see again, and let my sons see, the city of my childhood, which had suddenly become for me, now that she was dying, the city of my mother's youth.

The following summer, on a hot August day in 1984, the boys and I got on a plane in Paris and flew to Budapest. Michael was fourteen, already in his growth spurt, Daniel was seven: Mutt and Jeff, with Mom in between. As we got off the plane after an ordinary two-hour flight, I realized with a jolt that the journey it had taken me thirty-five years to embark on was shorter in actual time than the flight from Boston to Miami, which I had been making for years to visit my mother.

It was a fine vacation. We spent several days of a two-week stay (some of it outside Budapest) roaming the city, visiting the house and neighborhood where I had lived, taking many rolls of photographs. My sons shot pictures of me in the large cobblestoned courtyard where I had played as a child—shabby now, surrounded by pockmarked walls, with tufts of grass growing between the cobblestones; they snapped me on the fourth floor, leaning over the wrought iron banister in front of the apartment where I had lived with my parents and grandmother; they took snapshots of me on the steps of the *chupah*, the wedding canopy, in the courtyard of the synagogue where my parents were married (the synagogue itself was closed and boarded up). The same courtyard had been the recreation yard of my old religious school, now empty of children—it had become a kosher canteen for the elderly. In a curious way, I felt as if I had occupied all those places of my childhood so that I could return many years later and be photographed there by my children. I became, for a few days, a tour guide to my own life.

I told my sons about some of the memories stirred up by those stones and streets: the long Sunday walks with my mother and friends in the hills of Buda; scurrying to ballet lessons along crowded avenues in Pest on weekdays, accompanied by the Viennese lady I called Madame who taught me French; the visits to the pastry shop where they sold sugar cones filled with whipped chestnut cream in winter, thick and sweet and so smooth to the tongue. My sons listened, mildly interested, but I soon realized that for them this was not a nostalgia trip—they would have to reach their own middle age for that. In the meantime I had better not indulge too much in reminiscence.

The city lived on for me in the few fragments of autobiography I kept writing and rewriting after we returned home. In 1988 my mother died; a year later Hungary, like the rest of Eastern Europe, entered the post-Communist age. By the fall of 1991 a number of Hungarians were studying or spending fellowship years at Harvard, where I teach. Boundaries that once appeared uncrossable suddenly were no more; differences that once appeared absolute—between past and present, Hungarian and English, Budapest and Boston—were becoming blurred. I discovered, after more than ten years of living there, that the Boston area had a large community of Hungarian emigrants, some who had arrived soon after the war, others who came in 1956 or later. Some were Jewish survivors of Auschwitz or of the Budapest ghetto; a few were right-wing nationalists and anti-Semites who had fled Hungary with the German army at the end of the war. Between these two extremes were many ordinary people, who even after decades of living in the United States spoke English with a heavy accent and felt truly at home only with other Hungarians. Finally there were the temporary exiles, the students or postdoctoral fellows who were a good generation younger but with whom I often felt I had more in common because of our academic ties.

One day about that time, I received a letter with a Berlin postmark. It was from an institute for advanced study I had heard about, and it contained an invitation: Would I like to spend six months or a year in Budapest, as a fellow of a similar, newly founded institute? Providence *oblige*: I knew, as I read that letter from another world, that it carried a call I could not refuse. I had the vague but unshakable feeling that a radical turn in my life would occur if I returned again to my native city, only a few years after my mother's death. After some formal procedures on both ends, I was granted a semester's leave from Harvard and was officially declared a fellow of the Collegium Budapest Institute for Advanced Study, for six months beginning in February 1993.

I had a book to finish, and I did. But the writing project that became most compelling, most irresistible to me during my six months in Budapest was one I had not planned. From the first day on, no matter how late I got home, most nights I found myself in front of my computer, sometimes for hours, sometimes for only a few minutes, recording the events of the day—people I had met, things I had seen, heard, read. Many of my conversations were about politics, for the parliamentary elections were approaching; besides, everyone had an opinion about life after "the Change," as 1989 is referred to there. Had "the Change" brought greater hardship as well as freedom? And what about the rise of nationalism and anti-Semitism?

Although the bulk of this book consists of my 1993 Budapest diary (pruned and edited, with most of the names changed), it tells a much longer story—or maybe a more anonymous one, for it could belong to any number of people all over the world. It's the story of a woman's return, after many years of forgetfulness, to a city she once called home. Her peculiar relation to the city is best summed up as a relation to language: she speaks its language like a native, but with an accent. In the process of rediscovering the city as an adult—unforgetting what she once knew, learning what she never had a chance to know—she comes to experience it as home; but not *the* home, sentimentalized, found again at last. Rather, Budapest becomes one of the places where she feels at home, a city with a river running through it.

Is it the same city where she lived as a child? Yes and no. It has changed, and so has she; yet some things endure. One strand in her story is a quest for traces: traces of her childhood, the lives of her parents and their families, and the Jewish communities of Hungary and Poland. Sometimes her quest takes the form of visits to streets, houses, neighborhoods, cities; sometimes it is a hunt for copies of official documents—birth certificates, marriage certificates, death certificates. Documents are a sign of past existence, a form of memory; their absence may signal an attempt to eradicate, to pull up by the roots. In some Polish cities one can no longer find any documents certifying the birth, or death, of a single Jew.

The Hungarian term for copies of official documents translates literally into English as "excerpt from the motherbook." To a Hungarian ear those words are ordinary, prosaic; to my ear they are full of poetry. That highly poetic word *anyakönyv,* motherbook, evokes for me not only my mother or father. I also imagine it as an actual book, a great blank ledger in which we inscribe our lives—either literally, as I have attempted to do here, or metaphorically through the accumulation of choices, losses, and recoveries that constitute a life story, at once unique and part of a larger history.

1984: A BRIEF VACATION

In the taxi to our hotel, all I could think about was that I was in a city where even the cabdrivers spoke Hungarian. Once he found out I spoke the language and had lived in Budapest, our driver started firing questions: Where had I lived, when had I left, how old was I then, did I still have relatives here, how long were we staying? It made me uncomfortable, as if he were grilling me—I couldn't decide whether he was unusually nosy or merely observing some rule of hospitality unknown to me. I answered him in brief phrases, trying at the same time to look at the road we were traveling and to translate his questions for Michael and Daniel. The road from the airport, a stretch of ugly gray asphalt, could have been anywhere were it not for the occasional billboards in Hungarian. Michael and Daniel looked out the window, indifferent. What were they thinking? I wondered. Two weeks in Mom's old country—what a bore? Or what an adventure? I desperately wanted these sons of mine, to whom I had said so little about my childhood, to be interested in the city of my birth. Yet my own feelings were a jumble: excitement to be here, yes, but what else? I tried to muster up a feeling of nostalgia, without success.

As we got closer to the city, I could feel my heart beat faster. What would I remember? I had just turned ten when we left, a chubby little girl with thick braids who read a lot and felt awkward at ballet lessons. It was a whole world I had left behind, sights and sounds and smells that had blended long ago into a single multicolored block. Now I was back, a professor of French literature who could interpret intricate texts by Proust or Balzac but could not tell the difference, in Budapest, between friendly curiosity and invasive nosiness. It was as if a door had shut behind me when I left, sealing the first ten years of my life in an air-tight room. For thirty-five years I had managed not to give much thought to the room. What would happen now that I had turned the knob on the door?

"Would you like me to stop at Akácfa utca, so you can see the house where you lived?" It was the driver again, friendly, offering his contribution to my nostalgia. We had reached the city center, strangely quiet since it was a Sunday afternoon and all the stores were closed. There were almost no cars in the streets, and hardly any people on the sidewalks. I saw dark, ornate buildings and trolley tracks: a turn-of-the-century European capital with claims to greatness.

"It's not far out of our way," the driver said. All right, I told him, please drive by Akácfa utca; I'll show it to my kids. He turned onto a broad avenue, reached a corner with a yellow church, and pointed to the right. "There it is, Akácfa utca." *Utca* means street, *fa* means tree: Acacia Street. I looked down the street; it seemed anonymous, unfamiliar. I had lived there for ten years, the first decade of my life, and I didn't recognize a thing. The church surprised me, because I had always associated that neighborhood with Jewish things. "I lived at number 59,' I told the boys.

The driver swung the car around and headed toward the river.

I have always loved cities with rivers running through them. Budapest is like Rome or Paris, a great city defined by its river and bridges. We crossed a bridge above the grayish-green Danube. On both sides of us we could see other bridges in the distance. "They were all bombed during the war," the driver said. The one we were on was called Freedom Bridge; it had trolley tracks down the middle.

The Gellért Hotel rose before us, its stone terraces and

tall windows facing the river. A grand hotel, the Gellért, from another day. My mother had told me about its swimming pools, a place to go on fancy dates before the war. Now, like the whole city, it was slightly the worse for wear, but you couldn't tell that from the outside. "Tip generously," my uncle Lester had told me before we left. "When you get to the hotel, give something to the man at the desk." My uncle knew the Gellért well—he had returned to Budapest almost every summer for more than thirty years. "You'll never see better theater than in Budapest," he told me each time I saw him. Feeling awkward and self-conscious, I slipped two bills into the registration clerk's hand. He took them with a practiced gesture, acknowledging the gift with a slight smile. Whether for that or some other reason, we ended up in a huge rooom with a large balcony directly facing the Freedom Bridge. Stepping out onto the balcony, I noticed a grassy knoll next to the riverbank, with a statue on it: a monument to the Soviet army, a heroic soldier with arms upraised.

The next morning we took a formal tour of the city, complete with tourist bus and bilingual guide. This was highly unusual, since I never take such tours anywhere. Thinking back on it, I speculate about why I chose the most impersonal, most ritualized way to introduce my sons to the city of my birth. Did I want to affirm my own estrangement, confirm my feeling that I didn't remember anything? Or was it a native pride that pushed me, as if I wanted my sons to learn from an objective source the greatness of this capital, the beauty and variety of its sights? We trudged dutifully after our guide, an attractive woman in a red sundress, as she led us through the Church of King Mátyás, one of Hungary's great monarchs who reigned in the fifteenth century; after that she took us to the Basilica of Saint Stephen (too big and new for my taste) on the other side of the river. From the basilica we drove up People's Republic Avenue to Heroes' Square, in whose center is a procession of immense sculptures of men on horseback. Built in 1896 in honor of Hungary's thousandth birthday, our guide told us. Now the square was used for all the big parades; off to one side, barely visible, stood a massive statue of Lenin.

Our guide pointed out other sights from the bus, instructing us to be sure to go on the tour of the Parliament buildings and to visit the museum up in the castle, from whose terrace one could get an excellent view of the Parliament and the river and its bridges. The Chain Bridge in particular, the very first bridge built between Pest and Buda in the mid-nineteenth century, looked splendid from up there, she assured us. But Michael and Daniel said categorically, No more tour buses.

In the afternoon we discovered the Gellért's open-air pools, set in terraced grounds on the hillside. That's where my mother must have gone on her fancy dates, amid the inlaid colored tiles and smiling statues and stone vases. The main terrace was covered with deck chairs, almost all occupied by people talking loudly to their neighbors in Hungarian. Looking at those voluble, gesticulating men and women enjoying themselves in the sun, I recalled the lazy afternoons of my last summer in Hungary. We spent July and most of August of that year at my aunt's summer house near Budapest, on the shore of the Danube. The house was set in a large garden full of fruit trees and berry bushes: sour cherries that made your mouth pucker, thick clusters of gooseberries and red currants, sweet, fat apricots whose pits I broke open to reveal an edible almondlike center—all those riches reminded me of the fairy tales I loved, in which children in a magic forest find gingerbread and candy on the trees.

Every afternoon that summer, we went to the baths in a nearby village whose name means Star Mountain. The baths were a fancy establishment boasting three swimming pools and terraced lawns. Next to one of the pools was a café shaded by tall trees and sun umbrellas, serving cold drinks and sandwiches. There my parents sat with their friends, discussing the day's news and playing gin rummy while we children swam and jumped off the diving board feet first, noisily, over and over. Every once in a while I would run and peek at my father's cards, draping a wet arm around his neck and whispering to him self-importantly about the game. I loved hugging him. He was the handsomest man in that whole crowd, I told myself, with his high forehead and soft brown eyes, his rugged face transformed by a smile.

"Attention! The waves will start in three minutes. Attention, please! The waves will start in three minutes." The voice on the loudspeaker, imperious, broke into my thoughts and the conversations around us. Michael and Daniel immediately perked up, wanting to know what was going on. I realized the large pool in front of us was a wave pool, something I had never seen outside Hungary. Working in mysterious ways, a machine built into the pool churns up artificial waves for several minutes at a time. One of the pools at Star Mountain had been a wave pool— they would turn it on for fifteen minutes every hour, announcing it on the loudspeaker. No sooner had I explained this system to the boys than they were in the pool, delighted, standing immobile, waiting for the first wave to hit them. They jumped into it as if it were the ocean in Wellfleet, then came up sputtering, their mouths full of chlorinated water. Another try, successful this time, and they were launched: in they jumped, up they bobbed, over and over. "Hey, Mom! Come on in!" Watching their faces as they called to me, I had the feeling that this was their first truly impressive experience since we arrived in Budapest. I went into the pool and let them drag me under the next wave.

After that we had our routine: mornings doing what Mom wanted, afternoons at the wave pool, preferably for three or four sessions. One afternoon I left the boys by the pool and went shopping on my own. We had seen stores selling embroidered tablecloths and peasant blouses, but they were not what I wanted. I headed for a bookstore near Petőfi Sándor Street, named after the romantic poet who lost his life in the 1848 revolution. I bought a two-volume edition of Petőfi's complete works ("On your feet, Magyar, the homeland is calling you!" was the only line of Hungarian poetry I remembered); but the book I was really looking for was a children's novel by Ferenc Molnár, *The Boys from Paul Street*. When I first read that novel in Budapest, Molnár was a famous playwright living in New York, the author of the play the musical *Carousel* was based on. But I knew nothing about him other than his name on the cover of a book that made me cry and dream and imagine myself a heroic young boy fighting battles over a playground near a pond. The boys from Paul Street are a gang of adolescents warring with another gang over their turf. The story takes place around the turn of the century; the boys are not modern hoodlums with guns or knives, just old-fashioned schoolboys who fight with "bombs" made of sand (no rocks allowed). Still, theirs is a true war in the passions it arouses, and one of them even dies in heroic self-sacrifice: he spies on the opposing gang, jumps into the pond to avoid being seen, and stays in the cold water for several hours to help his friends—then dies of pneumonia.

Maybe because it was one of the last books I read before leaving Hungary, maybe also because its story had so much to do with home, and war, and death and loss, this novel stayed in my mind long after I had forgotten almost everything else I had read in Hungarian. Never mind that all the main characters were boys, I identified with them more memorably than I had ever done with a heroine. I had sometimes wondered, over the years, whether that book could still be bought in Budapest. Or was it no more than a fragment of the past, unreachable? Now I held it in my hand, a cheap paperback edition with a colorful cover, a children's classic. On the back of the title page, the original copyright date: 1907.

Over the next few afternoons by the wave pool, I succeeded in reading the book. It felt strange struggling over pages I had read with ease as a child. Curious existence, I told myself—professor in Boston, fourth-grader in Budapest. I tried to relive the emotions I had felt as a nine-year-old. It didn't work; no Time Recaptured here. But I did make one discovery: although I had cried over the death of the young sacrificial hero, it was not him I had identified with as a child. He was small and frail and caught cold easily. I took pride in being sturdy, in excellent health. I had identified with the leader of the gang, a tall, intelligent boy who survives.

As I was growing up, I often heard about my uncle Izsó, one of my mother's two bachelor brothers who were sent into forced labor in Ukraine around 1943. They had lived with us, and were both very fond of me. The younger one, Lester, showed up on the doorstep one morning in the spring of 1945 after our own return home, wearing a tattered army jacket and a week's beard, smiling broadly. Izsó, the older one, never came back. For years afterward my grandmother cried over her lost son. The one who had survived would shake his head and sigh: "Poor Izsó, he probably starved to death. He was too good. If only he had been with me, I could have saved him." Before, I had had three uncles (one in America). Now I had only two. What was the connection, I wondered, between goodness and survival?

A Brief Vacation

After a few days of sightseeing, I decided it was time to visit my old neighborhood. The boys loaded their cameras. We got on the streetcar in front of the Gellért, crossed the Freedom Bridge, and stayed on until the last stop. Walking for a while up People's Republic Avenue, we reached a busy intersection next to a leafy square named in honor of the composer Franz Liszt (Liszt Ferenc to Hungarians—last name first is the rule). A large, ornate building at the other end of the square turned out to be the Music Academy. It pleased me to have lived near music and greenery.

A short block away, we found Acacia Street and started our walk toward number 59. Everything looked alien on that gray, narrow, painfully run-down street. When we reached the house, we crossed to the other side to get a better view of it. The street level looked terrible: a heavy cement facing marred the facade, clashing with the stucco blocks above it. A large photography business occupied the whole width of the building and part of the next building as well. Above the front door, a large black- and- white sign proclaimed FOTO OPTIKA.

"This is not how it used to be," I told the boys, though I couldn't say just what had been there before. Looking up, I recognized the balcony next to our dining room, with its wrought iron railings. The house had only three balconies, arranged in a triangle; they stood out on the facade like signs of privilege. I had always felt a bit smug about our balcony. I pointed it out to my sons: that's where I had often played, looking down through the spaces between the railings at the people on the sidewalk. That's where we had set up the sukkah every year, the wooden hut used on Sukkoth, the Feast of Tabernacles, hanging homemade garlands of shiny colored paper and dried fruits and flowers on its walls in honor of the harvest.

Inside the building, the oblong courtyard looked familiar. How many games of tag I had played there after school! Its ground was cobblestoned, and there were bits of grass growing in the cracks. Standing in the center, surrounded by the wrought iron railings of the floors above, I had the feeling of being in an intricate cage. The wide stone staircase near the entrance also evoked memories. When I was in first grade, coming home from school I once saw a man on the landing who waited for me to approach, then quick as a flash opened his pants and pulled out something fleshy and pink. I ran past him, suffocating. By the time my mother and I returned to look for him, he was gone.

"No flasher here today," said Michael as we climbed up the three flights. We took a moment to catch our breath, and then I knocked on the door of the corner apartment. The door looked strangely out of place, but this was the right apartment. My heart was beating fast as we waited; after a few minutes, an elderly couple appeared. I explained who I was and asked if they would let me show the apartment to my children. "Come in," they said. We stepped into what used to be a large vestibule, with the kitchen off to the right. Now it was smaller, and to the right there was a wall. They had divided the apartment, the couple explained, giving part of it to their married daughter. That accounted for the strange shift in the front door—there were now two front doors, one to their apartment and one to hers.

We crossed the vestibule and entered the dining room, with its french doors leading to the balcony. There had been a large, heavy square table in the middle, which could seat more than twelve people for a seder. Now that space was empty. The grand piano had stood off to the right, and in the corner had been the green ceramic fireplace rising to the ceiling. Now there was a metal stove there. I asked about the green fireplace. "Yes, it was there at one time, but we had it replaced. This one heats better." They had been living in the apartment about twenty-five years. I thought of asking them to let us step out on the balcony but decided against it. Somehow, despite their friendliness, I felt we were intruders. Besides, there was nothing there of the home I had known. I thanked them with all the polite phrases I could muster as we left. Then my sons took pictures of me leaning over the railing opposite the front door, looking down into the courtyard.

Should I say I felt disappointed by this visit? No, I felt detached, like a tourist. I could not connect, in that moment, with the person I had been or with the meaning that home had once possessed for me.

Outside, we continued our walk. I tried to orient myself among that web of streets, where most of my daily life for ten years had unfolded: Dob Street, Klauzal Street, Kis Diófa Street, Kazinczy Street. The names sounded familiar, like a song learned in childhood, but the visual memory was gone. I remembered the synagogue on Kazinczy Street, in whose courtyard stood the *chupah,* the prescribed wedding canopy for Orthodox weddings that I had passed on my way to school every day. On ordinary days the framework of wrought iron remained uncovered, but for weddings it was covered with a roof of some silky material. In 1946 my second-grade teacher, a tall young woman with long brown hair, got married, and I was one of the pupils she chose as bridesmaids. I recently found a picture of the wedding in a box of old photos from my mother. I'm wrapped in a white fur coat that's too big for me, obviously borrowed. My hair is loose, as on festive occasions, with a large sausage curl on top and a white ribbon. The bride is also wearing a fur coat, open over her dark dress. She stands next to the groom under the canopy, surrounded by a crowd of men in black hats. The scene now strikes me as forlorn and poor, marked by the aftermath of war. Yet in the photo I look proud and happy, like someone starring in a grand event.

I turned six the summer after the war, just in time to start first grade at the normal age—as if all that had happened the previous year had been no more than a vivid nightmare, or one of the scary movies I loved and dreaded. My grandmother—small, round, vain, meddlesome, hovering—watched me leave for school every morning from the balcony above the street and waited there for my return at 1:00. If I was late, dawdling with the other girls, she would get anxious, then angry. One day when I had dawdled longer than usual (we were talking about sex), she scolded me loudly: she had been about to call the police when I showed up. I, big mouth, told her to stop acting like a policeman herself. Did she punish me for that freshness? No, she told the story of my clever repartee for years, to friends and family, anyone who would listen. "Clearly the child's a genius." That's how legends are born. That's why I forgave her all her meddling, because she loved me so much.

Each day after lunch, I would retire to the small desk in my room and open my primer. Learning to read was even better than noodles with plum jam, the most exciting, most deeply satisfying food I had ever tasted. The primer had a shiny hard cover. Inside, every page featured a particular letter or combination, in alphabetical order. The "star" letter was centered at the top of the page, very big, in color; below it a line of syllables, then a few lines of short words, then increasingly longer words down to the bottom. Throughout, the star letter was printed in color, so you always knew what you were learning. C (like the ts in "fits"), a big purple letter: ci, ca; cica, cat. Cs (like the ch in "macho"), in bright yellow: csi, csa; csak, only, kicsi, small, csillag, star. Sz (like the s in "sing"), a fiery red: szó, word, szólni, to speak to, szótár, dictionary. S (like sh), apple green: sok, much, soha, never, mese, story. Zs (like the j in

French "je"), royal blue: *zsu, zsa, zsi*; Zsuzsi, my name, Zsuzsika, its diminutive, a term of endearment, what my mother and grandmother called me.

I would spend hours at my desk, feeling happy as the afternoon wore on and I had to light the lamp. I've often heard people say Hungarian is an impossible language, too difficult for anyone to master who was not born into it. True, I was born into it, but Hungarian seemed to me the most wonderful, logical tongue in the world. Every consonant, alone or in combination with another, every vowel with or without an accent, has one sound only, no matter where it occurs. To learn to read, all you have to do is learn the sounds and put them together; after that you can read anything. But English, oh, English! *Bough, ought, rough, though. So, sow, sew*. Same letters, different sounds, same sound, different letters. How does any child here learn to read?

From the synagogue we went to visit Zsazsa Néni, my mother's aunt by marriage, who lived in the neighborhood. I had never heard of her until I began preparing for our trip—she was the widow of my mother's uncle, my grandfather's brother. My uncle Lester had given me some money to take to her; I had called her in the morning to say we were coming.

The woman who opened the door for us was tiny, spry, neatly dressed in a skirt and blouse, her dyed brown hair carefully combed. She was eighty-three but looked twenty years younger. "Zsuzsika! I've heard so much about you and your boys. Welcome!" she exclaimed. Only family called me Zsuzsika. I hugged her thin body, and so did the boys. We had wondered to ourselves how we should greet her, but now it seemed obvious. She led us into her living room, small and dark but very clean, furnished in what looked like art deco furniture from the time of her marriage. We sat on stiff chairs while she served us cold drinks and cookies. "Tell the boys to eat more," she urged me. I translated; the boys ate more.

Zsazsa Néni showed us a picture of her husband in an old photo album. In that formal portrait in sepia I recognized the Stern face, looking like my uncle Lester and like his brother Izsó who had died in forced labor: a round face framed by dark hair, serious, with horn-rimmed glasses. By an odd coincidence, this great-uncle's name was also Izsó, and he too had died in forced labor. Zsazsa Néni told the story matter-of-factly, stripped to its bare essentials. The rest of that branch of the family, cousins and siblings, parents and children, had perished at Auschwitz. A writer once told me that Holocaust survivors tend to speak (or even write) about their memories in clipped sentences, as if they were choking. Zsazsa Néni, for all her friendliness, fit the description.

We spoke about her life now. She was quite alone, having no children, and had been a widow since her husband died. She had worked in an office to support herself but had been retired for several years; she was living on a tiny pension, insufficient even for her very modest way of life. She took her hot meal at midday every day at the canteen on Kazinczy Street and received an American subsidy from my uncle Lester, her nephew.

She seemed to know a lot about me. My uncle had evidently bragged about the family honor ("Do you realize? A Harvard professor!"). He must also have told her about my divorce, for she discreetly made no mention of the children's father. We took her to lunch at the Gellért, where she found everything shockingly expensive. Before we left her house she gave me a present, a porcelain box in the shape of an egg, a lovely piece from Herend.

A few years later I heard from my uncle that she had had to give up the apartment and move into an old-age home; a few years after that she died. I wrote to her once, to send her photos the boys had taken of her. But I have a deplorable way of forgetting about people, as if once they were gone they had disappeared forever. Sometimes I think it's due to a first experience of abandonment during the war, when my survival depended on forgetting my mother. But that may be simply a convenient excuse for a basic lack of human connectedness, and I reproach myself for it. I still have the porcelain egg on my bookshelf, though. It is Zsazsa Néni's egg.

Among the things I didn't tell my sons while we were in Budapest were my memories of the last year of the war. I didn't consciously remain silent on that score; it simply didn't occur to me to talk about that year of my life, far back in early childhood. It was only after returning to Paris, emptied of Parisians in the late August heat (Michael and Daniel too were in the country) that I decided to write down the episodes I still carried with me from that year—fragmentary, incomplete, but possessing a vividness that surprised me. The experience of seeing again the places of my childhood had restored the sharpness of those images and revealed the desire, long suppressed, to put them into words.

What I wrote went like this:

They began rounding up the Jews in Budapest quite late in the war. June 1944; I was almost five years old.

We lived in an apartment building in a busy part of the city, not far from the Opera House. On the corner of our street stood a large yellow church; a few streets farther, the Orthodox synagogue and the Orthodox Community Bureau, where my father worked. Our apartment building had four stories, with a large inner courtyard bordered on each floor by a gallery with wrought iron railings. I would run up and down the gallery on our floor,

A Brief Vacation

and whenever I stopped and looked down into the courtyard, I felt dizzy. I held on to the railing, my heart pounding with excitement and fear, knowing all the while that I was safe. Then my grandmother would call me in for a snack of buttered bread, thickly sliced rye with a heavy crust, topped by a piece of salted green pepper. ("Oh, gross!" say my children—but they love green peppers. It must be in the blood.)

The night the Nazis came, about three or four in the morning, my mother woke me up and dressed me. She and my father and grandmother spoke in whispers, hurrying. After I was dressed, still half asleep, my mother took my hand and ran down the stairs with me. Or maybe she picked me up and ran, carrying me. She had torn the yellow star off her coat. At the bottom of the stairs we slowed down. There were soldiers on both sides of the street door, the concierge standing next to them—a plump, youngish woman, dressed in a heavy coat and felt slippers. It appeared that her job was to identify the Jewish tenants so none would leave the building on their own.

My mother and I walked past the concierge and the soldiers, out into the street where day was dawning. She held me tightly. We walked up the street toward the church, keeping a steady pace. Don't look as if you didn't belong here. After we had turned the corner, we started to run. A mad, panicked dash to the next corner, then a stop, out of breath. Saved.

I have never understood why the concierge let us go. Was she moved by the sight of the woman and child, or had my parents paid her off? Probably they had, for my father succeeded in skipping out a few minutes later. My grandmother stayed behind and was put in a place they called the ghetto, where she lived until the war was over. Later, when I told this story to my friends (everyone in first grade had a story, recounted with melodramatic flourishes on the way home from school), I found it miraculous that she was not taken to Auschwitz or lined up and shot into the Danube like the people another girl told about. It was at that time, I believe, that I began to conceive of history as a form of luck.

A Brief Vacation

The next scene takes place a few weeks after our escape from the house, on a farm far from Budapest. For safety my parents had decided to leave me with Christian farmers, as many other Jewish families were doing. My mother probably explained this to me, though I have no recollection of it. Nor do I remember actually arriving at the farm. I remember being there, scared.

The farmhouse kitchen had an earthen floor, with a long wooden table in the middle; in one corner stood a massive butter churn. I am standing next to the table with my mother and the farmer's wife. My mother has dressed me in a frilly dress and white leather shoes, like the ones I wear on afternoon visits in town. She kisses me and says it won't be for long. Then she leaves. I cry.

Now I am running across the large dust-covered yard, chased by geese. They are immense, honking furiously, wings aflutter. They're on my heels, stretching their necks to bite me. I run into the kitchen, screaming. The farmer's children laugh and call me a city girl. I can't stop crying and feel as if I will burn up with shame. As the tears stream down and smear my face, I make a promise to myself: they will not see me cry again.

How long did I stay on the farm? I don't know. It felt like a long time. It was summer, I must have turned five while I was there. Meanwhile, back in Budapest, my father managed to get false papers for all three of us. He and my mother decided to take me back, danger or no. By the time they came for me, I was used to the farm. My mother found me squatting in the dust with the other children, dressed only in panties, barefooted, busy playing with some broken bits of pottery. I hardly looked up when she ran to me and hugged me.

Thanks to our false papers, my parents found a job as caretakers on an estate in Buda. The owner of the estate was an old noblewoman, a sculptress. I have no visual memory of her, but I imagine her as a tall, thin, kindly lady with white hair—like the Old Lady in the story of Babar, which I read a few years later. According to my mother, the old lady became very fond of me, even invited my mother to give me an occasional bath in her bathtub. On most days my mother washed me while I stood in a small enamelware basin on the floor in our room. The room was so small that if I wasn't careful I would bump into the stove and burn myself. We had to make fires in the stove by then; it was autumn, turning cold.

My name was Mary. My mother whispered to me every morning not to forget it, never to say my real name, no matter who asked. I told her not to worry, I wouldn't tell. I felt grown-up and superior, carrying a secret like that.

Besides the old lady and us, four people lived in the house: the lady's young nephew, recently married, with his wife, and an older couple who were also caretakers of some kind. They had been with the lady for many years and were suspicious of us. One day they asked me what my mother's maiden name was. I said I didn't know, and told my mother. She told them not to ask me questions like that: Couldn't they see I was just a baby? Her maiden name was Stern, a Jewish name. I knew that name; it was my grandmother's. Luckily for us, I didn't know what "maiden name" meant.

When winter came more people arrived, relatives of the old lady. We all lived in one wing of the house to save heat. During the day the warmest place was the kitchen or a glass-enclosed veranda that received a great deal of sun. The lady's nephew and his wife spent all day on the veranda in wicker armchairs, reading or playing cards. I liked to watch them. The young man especially had a languid, almost petulant air that fascinated me. I recall him as tall and handsome. My mother said he was an "aristocrat," which I understood from her tone to mean something like "beautiful but weak." Watching him turn the pages of a book or run his fingers through his long, wavy hair, I felt totally infatuated; at the same time, perhaps because of my mother's intonation as she said the word "aristocrat," his gracefulness filled me with a kind of scorn.

For Christmas we decorated a tree. I sang "Holy Night" and

received presents. My mother had taught me the song during the whole month of December. There was a Christ child in a cradle under the tree. I was fascinated by the lifelike figure of the holy baby and by his mother's golden hair, but most of all I loved the shining colored globes and streams of glittering silver on the tree. Sometimes I felt sorry we weren't really Christians—we could have had a tree like that every year.

In January it turned bitter cold and snow fell. There were air raids at night, and we all started sleeping on cots in the basement. It soon became clear that my father was the man of the house. He made sure we all gathered in the basement during air raids, even during the day. He listened to the shortwave radio and told us when the Germans began retreating. When the pipes froze and we had no water, he organized our noctural expeditions to gather snow.

How can I describe those winter nights? For years they remained in my memory as an emblem of the war, of the immense adventure that, with hindsight and retelling, the war became for me. Picture a dozen shadows covered by white sheets, flitting across a snow-covered landscape. The sheets prevented our being seen from the air, blending with the white ground and trees. Mounds of soft snow, darkness, and silence—and with all that hushed beauty, a tingling sense of conspiracy. We carried pots and pans, scooping the cleanest snow into them with spoons. When a pot was full we took it inside, emptied it into a kettle on the stove, then went back to gather more. Three kettlefuls, my father said, would give us enough water for two days.

I don't know how many times we gathered snow, in fact. Maybe only twice, or once. No matter. I see myself triumphant, smug, impatient for the boiled snow to cool so that I can drink it. As I bring the glass to my lips, I meet my father's eyes. We exchange a look of pleasure. I am five years old, and I am drinking snow. Outside, bombs are falling. Here in the steamy kitchen, nothing can hurt me.

The Russians came a few weeks later. But first we had Ger-

A Brief Vacation

man guests. A detachment in retreat invaded the house and set up radio equipment in our kitchen. They were distant, polite, ordinary. I had imagined monsters, like Hitler. (Hitler had horns; he was a giant.) My mother prepared meals for them, listening to their talk—they had no idea she understood them. She would report their conversations to my father, but there was nothing new. Defeated or not, to us they were still a menace. After a few days they left. I felt extremely pleased with us, clever Davids outwitting Goliath.

A few nights later a bomb fell in our backyard. It made a terrific noise, and for a moment we thought it was the end. But when it turned out to have missed the house, we became quite jovial. As soon as there was enough daylight, we trooped out to inspect it. Whose bomb it was, we did not know; but there it sat, less than fifty meters from the house, in the middle of a crater it had made in landing, round and dark green like a watermelon. Somehow it all seemed like a joke, even though we kept repeating how lucky we were, how tragically ironic and ironically tragic it would have been to get killed when the war was almost over.

The Russians arrived huge and smiling, wrapped in large coats with fur on their heads. They were our liberators; we welcomed them. When they saw my father's gold watch, they laughed delightedly and asked for it. We didn't understand their words, but their gestures were clear. My father took off the watch and gave it to them. Then they asked my mother to go to their camp and cook for them. They put their arms around her, laughing. She pointed to me, laughing back and shaking her head. Who would take care of the little girl? They insisted, but she held fast. I felt frightened. Finally they let her go.

After that, everything becomes a blur. How much longer did we stay in the house? Did we ever tell the old lady who we were? She was sick, according to my mother, and died during the last days of the war. But I have no memory of that.

In 1945, sometime between March and May, we walked back to our house, crossing the Danube on a makeshift bridge. All the real *bridges had been blown up by the retreating Germans. Walking between my parents, holding each one's hand, I felt madly lucky and absolutely victorious, as if our survival had been wholly our doing and at the same time due entirely to chance. I was not aware of the paradox then or, if I was, could not have expressed it. But as I grow older, it occurs to me that I have often felt that way about my life: seeing it, for better or worse, as my own creation and at the same time, contradictorily, as the product of blind luck.*

That day I mostly stared and tried to register everything—storing it for future use, though I didn't know exactly what. I saw a dead horse lying on its side in the street, its legs stretched out; someone had cut a square hole in its flank for meat. From time to time a bombed-out wall showed where a house had been. We passed empty stores, their doors wide open—looted, said my mother. Inside one, on the floor in front of the counter, a white-haired woman lay dead. I couldn't take my eyes off her, despite my mother's pulling me away. Who had killed her? Did they do it for money? What did her skin feel like, now that she was dead? Was it cold and leathery? After a while I stopped thinking and even looking. I concentrated on putting one foot in front of the other.

On our street, all the houses were intact. We walked into ours through the downstairs door where the soldiers had stood a year before. The courtyard was covered with debris, and there were holes that looked like bullet holes in the walls. Up the stairs to the third landing: the lock on our apartment door was broken. Inside, the windows were all shattered. Dust lay over everything, stirred occasionally by a breeze. The sky through the glassless window frames looked so near you could almost touch it. I was no longer Mary, but for a moment I could not remember my name.

I saved the visit to the Buda hills for our last day. It was August 20, the Feast of Saint Stephen, a traditional holiday celebrating Hungary's first Christian monarch who reigned in the eleventh century. The Communist regime had taken over the tradition, emphasizing its nationalism minus the royalty. A water parade down the Danube was scheduled for 11:00 A.M, and in the afternoon there would be a military display with airplanes. The best part would be at night, a fireworks show over the water. I knew it would be spectacular because I remembered the one from the summer of 1949: fireworks exploding in the deep August sky in showers of green and gold and brilliant pink, while I lay on a blanket on a grassy terrace wishing it would never end. My parents had not yet told me we would be leaving Hungary, but the walls were thin in the summer house and I had heard them talking when they thought I was asleep. I slept badly that summer: too much to think about, too much to fear.

The boys and I decided to skip the parade but to be back in time for the fireworks. The view from the square in front of the hotel would be perfect, the porter assured us as we left for the hills.

Every Sunday after the war, from fall to late spring, my mother would wake me early, even earlier than on a schoolday. Sometimes we would leave the house when it was still dark, carrying walking sticks and knapsacks containing our lunch; in the winter we would also take a sled, carrying it or pulling it behind us if there was snow on the sidewalk. To get to our mountain we had to take a streetcar to the cog railway, then sit in one of the ancient, swaying carriages as it slowly made its way up on spoked wheels. We would meet friends at the railway, other families with children, then crowd into the carriage and rush for seats on its wooden benches. At the top, we would pile out and take deep breaths of "pure mountain air," as my mother liked to say—she was a lifelong believer in the restorative powers of fresh air.

Below us was a wide, open slope overlooking the city, bordered by a row of trees at the bottom; beyond the trees lay another slope, but we kept to ours. In autumn we children would run around in the crisp morning light, playing tag or hide-and-seek among the trees and gathering wild chestnuts (the most prized were shiny, reddish brown, and perfectly round) or bouquets of colored leaves. In spring we would pick wildflowers while the grown-ups sat and gossiped.

But my favorite season was winter; our slope was always covered with a deep layer of snow, perfect for sledding. We would slide down to the row of trees, two or three on a sled, then huff and puff our way back up, pulling the sled by a rope. Often the grown-ups joined us for those slides. I really loved my mother then; she was always willing to go for one more ride. I sat behind her on the sled, hugging her waist and burying my face in her coat. "Hang on!" she cried, and down we sped, screaming with pleasure and fear as we neared the trees. With an expert tug she steered the sled to a stop a safe distance from the tree line; then we struggled back up and started over.

When we were tired out or chilled to the bone, we went inside the big wooden shelter lined with picnic tables and unpacked our knapsacks. Soon the table was covered with food, shared among all: cold roast chicken, hard-boiled eggs, green peppers cut into large flat pieces accompanied by little paper cones of salt, apples and oranges and poppyseed pastry, or else crescents filled with apricot jam or crushed walnuts and sugar. Presiding over the feast, like majordomos, were the tall thermoses filled with sweet, hot lemon tea. *Hot lemon tea burning my mouth*, exquisite days of friendship and laughter.

After lunch, we would pack up the remaining food and get ready for the long walk down. Well-worn paths, covered with leaves or mud or snow: we children would run ahead, clambering over rocks, then circle back to where the grown-ups were trudging with their walking sticks. By the time we reached the bottom it was often turning dark—time to hurry home, to dinner and the lamp and a new week, until the next Sunday outing.

One thing bothered me on those perfect days: my father was almost never with us. The other families usually had both parents along: Why not us? The simple answer was that my father had to work. Since the Orthodox Community Bureau closed every Friday afternoon and all day Saturday in observance of the Sabbath, as well as on all the Jewish holidays throughout the year, an ordinary Sunday was a working day. My father, who had increasingly heavy responsibilities in the running of the Bureau, was obliged to be there. I suspected, however, that there was a less avowable reason as well for his never accompanying us on our hikes. They gave him a chance to spend a peaceful day by himself, away from the daily quarrels with my mother. The tragic truth about our family, I discovered as I grew up, was that my parents hated each other—at least that's how it appeared to me. Morally, intellectually, spiritually, they lived on different planets; and since both were strong-willed, neither could let the other's difference simply be. Theirs were not the quarrels I've sometimes seen between happily married people, quick outbursts followed by long periods of calm and harmony. They fought like gladiators, out for the kill.

The usual arena for their quarrels was our midday meal: it would begin calmly enough, after I returned from school. We would sit around the dining room table, my parents and I and my grandmother, often joined by my uncle Lester, who respected his mother. The food, cooked by my grandmother, was delicious, especially the noodle dishes she made because she knew I loved them: fat dumplings stuffed with plum jam, small sausage-shaped noodles sautéed with breadcrumbs, thin squares of dough fried with cabbage and onions, or simply the *nockerli* that went with chicken paprikas. I would throw myself on the heaping dishes, hoping no fight would break out if I ate with gusto. Right after the war, many of the fights had concerned my lack of appetite—everyone agreed I was too scrawny, but opinions were sharply divided about how to get me to eat more, and what to make me eat. My grandmother and uncle often joined in, arguing over whether to force me to take cod-liver oil, a horrible concoction I hated. I no longer recall who was on the laissez-faire side and who on the "force for her own good" side. Maybe they took turns, but the hard line must have won out often; I can still recall the forcible entry of the spoon and the foul taste of the cod-liver oil before I spit it out, crying and sputtering.

Alternating with these scenes of force were the desperate games my parents invented, at which my father excelled. Cut the meat into small pieces, then sing a song: "Watch the birdie! Open your mouth and watch the birdie fly into it!" Wham, another piece swallowed. The game could last half an hour or more, just to get me to eat when I wasn't hungry.

Many years later, as an overweight teenager in Chicago, I would curse those early stuffing sessions that had turned me into a fat little girl and fight violently with my mother, who could not stop nagging me about my weight. In Budapest, however, the fights were between my parents. First about my skinniness, then after they had fattened me up, over everything and nothing, with a violence far surpassing any possible cause. It terrified me. He never hit her, as far as I recall. But the verbal passion and abuse on both sides were so strong that for years I was convinced family life, and even family love, could not exist without yelling and wounding by words. "Galizianer! Go back to the slum where you grew up!" my mother would scream. "Hysterical woman!" my father would scream back (he was not as imaginative in invective). One or both of them would then leave the table, upsetting their chairs and slamming the door behind them. I would continue to stuff my mouth with noodles while my grandmother wrung her hands. The maid would come in to clear the dishes: the midday meal was over.

Yet it had been a marriage of love—certainly on my father's part, for he had braved his own father's wrath by marrying a girl without a dowry, two years older than himself. My father came from a family of Polish immigrants out of Galicia, reputed to be the region where the poorest Jews lived, the only son among four daughters. His father, though only a tailor with hardly any formal education, had a strong sense of his own dignity: a *cohen,* a member of the priestly class, he was among those called to the front of the synagogue on the High Holidays to bless the congregation. Besides, he was a devout, God-fearing man; he sent his only son, a *cohen* like himself, to an ultra-Orthodox yeshiva in the provinces to keep him away from the temptations of the big city. He hoped the boy would become a great Talmudic scholar and marry a rabbi's daughter, after which he could become a rabbi himself. It strikes me as mildly comical that even for that Chasidic line of work you needed connections to get ahead. Rabbinical families were dynasties: one had to be born or marry into them.

My father became a brilliant Talmudic scholar and fulfilled all the requirements to be a rabbi—all except one, for he refused to marry the girl his father had picked out for him. His father cursed him for his stubbornness, the missed opportunity; but by then he was in love with my mother, and nothing would budge him.

They had met at the Orthodox Community Bureau in the early thirties, when he was just starting out; she was a cashier in one of the kosher butcher shops, and it was to him she brought the receipts each day after closing. My mother was beautiful, with luxuriant dark brown hair and the bluest eyes imaginable. She knew how to flirt, too, especially with a yeshiva boy fresh out of school and not bad-looking himself. She wore lipstick and stylish clothes, unlike the rabbi's daughter. I think my father also loved her being well versed in the ways of the city. Their daily flirtation soon led to clandestine dates, and eventually to a clandestine marriage; they were legally married for over two years, each living at home as if nothing had changed, before he dared to tell his family and have a proper religious wedding. His mother and sisters prepared for the wedding, but his father had to be cajoled and refused to attend until the last minute. He finally went, but he never did sanction his son's misalliance.

Actually, it was considered a misalliance by both sides; my mother's family, though not as outraged by the marriage as his, had at one time harbored higher ambitions. They had been wealthy merchants in the dry-goods business, observant Jews who were proud of their culture in opera and theater, their perfect knowledge of Hungarian and their fluent German (my father's parents spoke Yiddish at home), their friendships with university graduates and members of the liberal professions. The family fell from grace when my grandfather died of a stroke while still in his forties, leaving his widow with six young children and no trustworthy financial adviser. By the time my mother reached marrying age, the family was almost penniless. That's why she had to work as a cashier, and why the young man she was madly in love with when she was twenty could not marry her, though he loved her just as madly. His parents, who owned a grocery store, would not waste their only son on a girl without a dowry.

She met my father on the rebound, found him attractive, and married him. She knew he was crazy about her; he saved her from the dreaded fate of spinsterhood, assigned in her mind to any unmarried woman over twenty-five. He

had the additional virtue of satisfying her sexually, as I discovered shortly after we left Hungary. One night when we
shared a hotel room in Vienna, I heard them making
cooing love talk, in voices I never heard during the day.
"Do you love my little beehive?" she crooned. "Yes I do, I
do," he crooned back. How could they hate each other
during the day and love each other passionately at night?
That mystery bothered me for years.

Before they married she had promised to keep an Orthodox home, and she kept that promise. In our house no
lights were turned on on the Sabbath except by the Christian maid; the kitchen was strictly kosher, and all the holidays were scrupulously observed. Once a month my
mother went to the mikvah, the women's ritual bath, to
cleanse herself after her period as prescribed by the Law.
But she would not cut off her hair and wear a *shaytl*, the
wig of Orthodox married women, as my father had hoped
she would; and later, in their fights, she taunted him for being a Galizianer from the Yiddish-speaking slums. In fact,
by the time he married her his family no longer lived in the
slums, owing to a daughter's success in business; but facts
were irrelevant to my mother's insults. He in turn blamed
her for never trying to make peace with his father (she felt
her father-in-law despised her), never understanding his
own spiritual needs.

All this I pieced together much later. My mother told me
about her first love, Ernö Farkas, during our long drive
east from Chicago after my father died of a heart attack,
the summer I turned twenty. I was still in shock from the
suddenness of his death, although he had been a sick man
ever since his first heart attack in Budapest. I told myself,
in a moment of bitterness, that dying at age forty-nine had
been his way of putting a definitive end to family life with
my mother. As for Ernö Farkas, he and his parents died at

A Brief Vacation

Auschwitz. "Maybe if I had married him, I would be dead too," my mother commented as she told me the story.

Other facts I learned recently from my aunts, my father's sisters, three of whom are still living in Toronto. It was they who told me the story of my grandfather, how he had emigrated from a small town in Galicia around 1900 while still in his teens, penniless and an orphan, and returned years later to his hometown to find a wife; how he had learned the tailor's trade and prospered for a number of years in Budapest making work clothes, before business turned bad; how proud a man and unforgiving a father he had been, refusing to bless his only son's marriage.

Few children know the stories of their parents. During my childhood, I knew only that mine were an impossible match—which did not prevent my mother from spending day and night at my father's bedside after his first heart attack, or from cutting off her beautiful hair as a propitiatory offering to the Orthodox God for allowing him to get well. Her hair grew back, and their quarrels resumed. I felt caught between them. All my life, I felt, I would have to choose one or the other, one over the other—soulful intellectualism or down-to-earth vitality, the harmonious union I yearned for forever beyond my grasp.

So our Sunday excursions to the Buda hills, which I thought of for many years as my mother's greatest legacy, had their dark side. Yet they remained in my memory as moments of pure grace and happiness, what I imagine Hegel must have meant by his poetic phrase "the Sunday of life." I first read that phrase in graduate school, in a French novel by that title. I have often thought that if I were to write about those years in Budapest after the war, years when the excursions to the Buda hills occupied such an important place in my life, I would use the same title.

It was indeed the Sunday of life, even on weekdays, for the lucky little girl who had survived the war with both her parents and her grandmother and one uncle. After school, she and Madame always stopped at the pastry shop to buy cones filled with chestnut cream; at home Madame helped her practice the piano, learning scales and Strauss waltzes. Sometimes a seamstress came to the house to measure her for flannel pajamas and everyday dresses. Her fancy dresses were made by a designer in the city who specialized in girls' clothing—clearly her mother denied her nothing. Before long the word "bourgeois" would become a term of insult and reprobation in her country; but for a few charmed years, the discreet pleasures of bourgeois existence in a great capital shielded her from life's hardships and helped to heal, perhaps, the scars inflicted by the war.

I thought about all this while sitting next to Michael and Daniel in the streetcar to the cog railway, which the hotel porter had told us was still in service. The boys were eager to see the spoked wheels and the rickety wooden seats—like the wave pool, a cool experience found only in Budapest. At the station we bought our tickets for the top, then waited for the train. It arrived, shiny, red, its spoked wheels hidden: inside, the seats were of fake leather and looked spanking new. "The old one must have worn out," I told the boys apologetically.

As the train wound its way up, making frequent stops, I began to feel anxious. The view from the windows was of suburban bungalows set amid neat lawns and gardens. Inside the carriage, our fellow travelers looked more like commuters going home than like hikers striking out for the wild. Had the open vistas and sledding slopes, the wooded trails that made you feel far from the inhabited world, all that verdant wilderness, been turned into a vulgar suburb? "Terminus!" I heard the conductor cry. We had to get off, and we saw only more houses, more lawns. In desperation, I stopped a woman walking near us. "Excuse me, isn't there a place near here for hiking? A mountain?"

"Follow those people," she said. "You have to take the Úttörö train; get off at the first stop."

Úttörö, the Young Pioneers—we wore navy blue skirts, white blouses, red string ties. Everybody in my fourth-grade class belonged to the Communist scouts—it was obligatory. I put my whole heart and soul into it; at the end-of-year school ceremony, I recited one of Petöfi's inflammatory poems against the monarchy, hammering its refrain: "Hang all kings!" The Úttörö train had been inaugurated that same year, a miniature railway run entirely by members of the Young Pioneers.

The boys and I followed the people in front of us about a block or two, then saw the uniformed conductor, who looked about twelve years old. We rushed to buy our tickets at the ticket window, ran for the train, and got on just before it started to move. At the first stop, we got off as the woman had instructed us. Still no wilderness in sight, but a big sign with an arrow pointed to "Normafa." Yes, I knew that name. We half ran in the direction of the arrow, past some houses, around the corner: there in front of us was the slope with its row of trees at the bottom, a wide-open panorama of the city and of other mountains in the distance.

Here was my *temps retrouvé* at last, only a little the worse for wear (I could hear buses on a hidden road to our left; there was evidently no need to take all those trains to get here). We ate our picnic lunch, cold chicken sandwiches and hard-boiled eggs courtesy of the Gellért, on a bench overlooking the vista. "The trees are still there," I said to the boys. "Why shouldn't they be?" they answered. Then they ran around for a while, and after that we took photographs. Michael took one of me standing in front of a trail sign with the word "Normafa" in big block letters, smiling broadly.

My thrill at finding those trees was like the thrill of find-

ing *The Boys from Paul Street* in the first bookstore, a magi-
cal piece of childhood incarnate. Had I really expected the
trees to be gone, the novel to have disappeared as if they
had never existed? I think so, or at least I feared the worst.
My sons' reaction was more practical: Why shouldn't the
trees be there? I tell myself that may be the difference between a secure childhood and an insecure one. Maybe
that's too easy.

That evening we watched the fireworks in the middle of
a noisy crowd in front of the Gellért. Brilliant bursts of
color rising like giant fountains, then falling back in fading
showers over the Danube. Daniel, as his only entry in our
travel diary, wrote that night in his seven-year-old's scrawl:
"We saw fireworks that went high high up and then came
down again and there was a big Greek fire at the end."
Thirty-five years earlier, I had lain on the grass above the
swimming pool in Star Mountain, watching those same
bursts of color, wondering what the future would bring.
One thing it had brought was motherhood, these two sons
I loved more than anyone else on earth. It had also brought
this brief vacation in Budapest, a return after much movement: Vienna, Munich, Paris (repeatedly, punctuating my
life like a heartbeat), Port-au-Prince, New York, Chicago,
Cambridge, New York again, Los Angeles, Princeton,
Cambridge again. Different cities, different languages,
different worlds, each one feeling like home—for a while.

The image of a children's game keeps coming back to
me: the French call it *saute-mouton,* "jump-sheep." In English it's leapfrog. Woolly white fat sheep, gamboling
across a field near the Loire. Wise old slimy frogs, kicking
their legs and croaking as they cross a pond in Georgia, or
Sussex. But the lines get crossed, for "frog" can mean
Frenchman, and *mouton* is that most English of foods, mut-
ton. (The tender lamb of an elegant *gigot* is not *mouton,* but
agneau.) More to the point, *mouton* also means passive vic-

tim, as in English: sheep to the slaughter. I ask myself, Does that happy image of the *saute-mouton* screen a more angry, painful memory? Jews in long rows, marching. . . . No, not that now. Now concentrate on this: I know about "frog" and *mouton* without opening a dictionary. To find the equivalent in Hungarian would take me hours in a library. I have no idea which animals leap on the Hungarian plain, or whether any leap at all.

Between the ages of six and eleven, I learned to read and write three different languages in four countries. Each new language was not so much an addition as a replacement; each new country a home to replace one left behind. The emigrant, always leaving one home or another, learns quickly that it does not pay to look back. She learns to adjust to each new place as if it were the last stop, even if she knows it is only a way station. Occasionally she remembers the first: the mother tongue, the home she left that did not replace anything. If she is lucky, she has a chance many years later to return there with her children, becoming for a few days the tour guide to her life. If she is very lucky she will return again. She will remember a book about boys fighting for a playground, a sun-filled apartment above an oblong courtyard, cobblestoned.

1993: BUDAPEST DIARY

Through a Stranger's Eyes

Boston last night, Budapest this morning—talk about a world of difference! But let's not jump to conclusions.

I was met at the airport by Trevor, a young American who works at the Collegium. He told me he came to Budapest two years ago on a study-abroad program, learned Hungarian, and decided to stay awhile. His job is that of liaison for the fellows at the Collegium. He has a Hungarian girlfriend.

I tried to pay attention as we drove toward the city, but things went by in a blur. I did sit up when we crossed the Freedom Bridge and passed the Gellért Hotel. A few minutes later we arrived at Ulászló Street. Number 49 is a three-story building of prewar vintage, with a small garden in front; my apartment is the whole top floor. It feels very quiet, as if no one else were in the house. Trevor helped carry my bags up. After he left I started to unpack but wasn't in the mood. I walked around the apartment: shiny hardwood floors, plenty of light. The living room furniture is comfortable, not elegant, though it tries to gesture in that direction. The sofa and armchairs are covered in an ugly flowered cotton, mostly dark green, and lace doilies peek out from under some cut crystal vases. Large TV set, CD player.

I didn't want to sleep in the middle of the afternoon, so after taking a hot bath and changing clothes I went to the Collegium. I walked part of the way, down toward the Gellért on Bartók Béla Avenue, a wide, busy street lined with shops. I stopped at one to buy a toothbrush; it felt strange to be speaking Hungarian to the young woman in the store. I thought I was speaking badly, like a foreigner.

Budapest Diary

The Collegium is in a beautiful eighteenth-century building, newly renovated, up on Castle Hill, across the square from the Mátyás Church, which looks positively dreamlike lit up in the evening. Trevor was still around, and he introduced me to Tibor, a fellow from Paris who's actually a Hungarian (left in 1956), and to Stanislaw, whom everyone calls Stani, a Polish writer. I also met a young French geographer whose office is next to mine. She invited me for a drink with some people in the bar across the street. By then I was beginning to feel dizzy with fatigue, and I followed the conversation as if in a fog. Following Trevor's instructions, I walked down the hill past the Hilton, and after stopping to buy some tea and a kind of open-faced sandwich in a twenty-four-hour store, I took a taxi home.

Alone, and feeling lonely.

FRIDAY, FEBRUARY 5

Had a chat with the downstairs neighbor this morning, a woman in her sixties I'd guess. She and her husband have been living in this house for over thirty years. It was a state-owned building, but three years ago the tenants were given the option to buy their apartments. They all had their places redone inside, but they have no money left to repair the outside, which still bears shrapnel holes from the war. There are six apartments in the building. Most were divided and are smaller than mine.

Shall I go back to Acacia Street and climb again the three flights of stairs to our old apartment, now divided? Maybe the couple who were there nine years ago no longer live there, or maybe they've bought the place and had it redone.

After lunch at the Collegium, I took a taxi to the home of János, one of the editors of a recently founded monthly journal, whose name was on my list of people to call. He had told me on the telephone yesterday that he lived in an old-style building with galleries surrounding the court-yard and asked whether I was afraid of heights. No I wasn't, I assured him—and a good thing, too, because his gallery is very narrow and from the third floor where he lives one has a plunging view. The building reminded me of Acacia Street, but it was not as nice—narrow galleries, no wrought iron, a smallish courtyard full of parked cars.

The man who opened the door was tall, about fifty, pleasant face, almost bald, and what hair he had was white. The apartment's clutter matched the exterior mess. He invited me into the tiny kitchen while he made coffee. He has a very charming, informal manner and a boyish air that I suspect he cultivates. After the coffee was made, he invited me into his study, a large, pleasant room lined with books that we reached through a small bathroom. His computer was still on, and he showed me the database he's been working on for the past fifteen years, just finished: a complete catalog, in French, of Hungarian poetry written before 1600. A true work of erudition, which somehow didn't fit in my mind with his image as an editor of a chic journal. But János turned out to be a man of many interests and talents ("My 'violon d'Ingres' is a whole orchestra," he joked, punning on the French term for "hobby"), and we spent a pleasant few hours talking about everything from opera to French structuralism, with which he feels a great affinity. At first we spoke Hungarian, but when things got really interesting we settled into French, which he speaks fluently with a heavy accent.

I asked him about the journal. "Well, I think you have great areas of empathy in you, but you simply cannot imagine what it was like to be an intellectual here around 1987–88. Suddenly, everything seemed possible. I had pur-posely chosen to specialize in literature before 1600, just to make sure I'd never have to write anything about politics. Under the Communist regime, that was the only way I felt I could survive. But then, when things began to change, I decided to take an active role." So he and some friends founded the journal, in the very room where we were sitting—and he didn't even have a phone at the time!

After looking at the contents page of my book *Subversive Intent*, which I had photocopied for him, he asked: "Are you close to feminism?"

"Yes," I answered.

He smiled broadly: "I wrote one of the first feminist articles in Hungary—about a sixteenth-century poet, the first Hungarian woman poet, who wasn't mentioned in any of the official literary histories." But now he no longer considers himself a feminist because all the ones he knows are too angry. He likes women, but not feminism.

"Are there any women on the editorial board of your journal?" I asked. I knew full well there weren't; I had read the masthead.

"No, and I'll tell you why. There are a lot of 'fistfights' among the editors, and a woman's presence would change that. Some men become too wildly competitive if a woman's in the room, to prove themselves to her. What do you think about that?"

"That it's very hard for men to think of women as equals."

He gave me his latest book—about three kinds of readers, all of them "played" by himself. As he was telling me about his three readers I couldn't help thinking of the four sons at the seder, especially since he had mentioned a short while before that both of his paternal grandparents were Jewish. He said that he and his father never thought of themselves as Jews, though at the first sign of anti-Semitism he identifies himself as one. He inscribed his book, in Hungarian, "To Zsuzsa, with much affection—János the feminist." I gave him some of my essays. The visit lasted more than four hours.

SATURDAY, FEBRUARY 6

Went out to buy some groceries this morning. It was a gray, sunless day, and I noticed once again how drably people were dressed. I was aware of women looking me over as I walked by, wearing a long green skirt and winter jacket, with suede boots. The eyes of those women dressed in gray or black weren't kind. "I stick out here like a sore thumb," I said to myself. I much preferred the area near Andrássy Avenue where János lives, even if the air is as bad in Pest as everyone says (he too said it yesterday). If it's so bad, why do people like him live there?

Spent the afternoon in my office at the Collegium, reading final papers for my "War and Memory" seminar at Harvard. The first one I read was a young woman's interview with her father, about the last year of the war he spent in Budapest. He's older than I am; he was eight years old in the harsh winter of 1944–45 when all the fighting was going on. Many parallels between our stories, including that all of his immediate family survived. The daughter writes that she has always known her father was a Holocaust survivor, and he told her many stories when she was a child. But the stories were always doctored so they were tales of good luck and triumph, not of fear or anxiety. It was only now, in this formal interview, that her father, with her prompting, spoke about his fears.

Reading her essay, I wondered why I never told such stories to my children—why, in innocence or thoughtlessness, I never considered myself a survivor all these years. I think it's because I left Hungary in 1949, not in 1956 like this student's father. He was twenty in 1956, a grown man, and he still speaks English with an accent—there was no

57

forgetting his past. Those few years made all the difference. By the time I graduated from high school I looked and spoke like any other middle-class American Jewish girl from a big city, so I could easily pass, forget where I came from or consider it irrelevant. Yes, I ended up studying French and became bilingual in French—but that was still a slanted way of acknowledging my past, since France for me is a country of choice, not of origin.

The funny thing is, these days I'm irritated to discover that an acquaintance is unaware of my background, considering me "an ordinary American." Last week, at a dinner in Cambridge, a colleague I've known for years expressed surprise when I told her I was born in Budapest. I could hardly wait to get home so I could send her my "war memoir" and set the record straight!

Two days ago I bought *Magyar Forum*, a weekly newspaper linked to the ruling party, the MDF—or rather, to the party's far-right wing, led by one István Csurka. Csurka writes a full-page article every week, and I finally read it this morning—a piece extolling the Hungarian people (*Magyar nép*), the "silent majority" against the political "elite." Since the article starts out by talking about a former head of the national bank who was mixed up in some scandal and who "has an Israeli passport," "elite" may be a code word for Jews. A pretty piece of populist rhetoric, on the whole. I imagine it's the sort of thing that would appeal to the woman in the grocery store this morning whom I overheard complaining about the price of life: everything was becoming unaffordable by ordinary folk, she told a man while standing in line to pay. But maybe I'm jumping to conclusions about the poor lady.

This evening I went to a free concert at the French Institute: a recital by the pianist Zoltán Kocsis. Big, appreciative audience—it felt good to be in a "culture crowd" in

Through a Stranger's Eyes

Budapest. Interesting how certain groups remain the same, no matter where you are or what language is spoken around you. Whenever I'm in a university, I feel in a familiar place, even if it's physically different from an American campus. The same with tonight's concert hall—it was comforting. I've been feeling lonely, and the weather is no help with so little sun. Evening falls much earlier than in Boston, around 4:00 P.M., and there's often a fog above the river. Tonight after the concert I walked along the Danube bank on the Buda side, from the Chain Bridge to Elizabeth Bridge. I passed some taxis in front of the casino, a small, lit-up building standing all by itself near Elizabeth Bridge. Walking on, I suddenly felt uncomfortable because I noticed I was now below the bridge, next to a kind of highway, with very few cars and no taxis passing, and nobody on foot either. So I circled back toward where I saw more cars and found myself once again near the casino. I took one of the taxis and was home in a few minutes.

MONDAY, FEBRUARY 8

I feel better about my neighborhood. The Collegium's rector assured me at dinner last night (official dinner for the fellows) that it's perfectly safe, and the apartment is wonderfully roomy and comfortable.

People in this city can be awfully touchy. A few days ago I stopped to buy some shampoo in a small store on the avenue, which was crowded with customers. A young woman near the cash register was surveying the clients, and at one point she said to a woman, "Don't handle the merchandise too much." The woman got terribly upset and stalked out of the store without buying anything: "You're too disrespectful [pimasz], so I won't buy from you," she said in a huff. Similar scene the next day at the flower vendor's stall on the corner of Bartók Béla and

59

Bocskai Avenues. The old lady told a young woman not to handle the flowers, and the woman went away saying "Then I won't buy any." Finally, a similar scene at the concert at the French Institute on Saturday night. During intermission, many people were milling around the bar ordering coffee, tea, or other drinks. A young man calls out to the waitress: "One coffee, please." His friend, another young guy, adds, "some cream" and then, "one milk." The waitress thought he was ordering a glass of milk, which was a little strange for that time of night for a young adult. She was about to give it to him when he said, very rudely, "Didn't you understand I was asking for milk in my coffee?"

"But you didn't say that, you didn't say 'a coffee with milk.'"

"Well, you heard me ask for cream, didn't you? What did you think I wanted to do with it, pour it behind my ear?"

At that point she got very angry and threw his change on the counter. He grumbled, "You don't have to throw things at me, madam."

The scene was imbued with a degree of aggression I found astonishing, directed largely by the young man at the young woman. In the other scenes two women were involved each time, so it's not a gender issue, though here I think there was some of that as well. What to conclude? That Hungarians have easily bruised egos? That under the new democratic regime, they won't "let themselves be pushed around anymore"? Or perhaps that they're feeling generally anxious, especially about things related to money.

Another thing I've noticed: toilets here have a strange shape on the inside. Instead of sloping so that the shit or piss hits the water in the basin, they have a porcelain platform that receives the stuff like a plate. So when you pee or shit and then get up and turn around, you can see what you made neatly displayed on the white platter below you, waiting for you to pull the flush. It reminds me of the way toddlers being toilet trained display their "products" to the general ohing and ahing of their families. (I have vague memories of Mother praising me for the wonderful "thing I had made" when I was about two years old.) In Budapest, even adults can admire their own excretions every time they go to the bathroom. Doubtless they would find our American toilets weird, swallowing everything up.

TUESDAY, FEBRUARY 9

Very interesting TV program this evening—the first of two documentaries on the political history of Hungary from the 1930s to 1956, as seen from the viewpoint of three men who were in their twenties during the war and later left the country. They all talked about the war: by 1944, when the Germans occupied Hungary, it was time to resist. One, a big bearded fellow, told a good story. He and some other students composed a text protesting the German occupation (March 1944), and their plan was to have it posted all over the city. The plan was never realized because the young man carrying the text to the printer was arrested by the Hungarian secret police. But nobody got hurt or even thrown in prison, because the police chief found out that not a single Communist or Jew had been among the plotters. "You understand, the myth was that only Communists and Jews were resisting Hitler—no authentic Hungarian would dream of such a thing. They preferred to hush up the whole affair rather than have to admit the truth." And he gave a big laugh.

After the war all three men were involved in a democratic alliance, and their story is essentially the story of how Mátyás Rákosi and the Communists succeeded in taking over the country. There was documentary footage of mass demonstrations of the time, huge crowds gathered on Heroes' Square, addressed by Rákosi and other orators. In one, around 1947, just before the elections that brought the Communists to power, people chanted "Long live Stalin!" and carried huge photos of him on banners floating above the crowd. Did I see crowds like that? For many people the Soviets still appeared heroic in those days—their army had, after all, liberated Hungary from the Nazis.

The film ended with a group of children, boys and girls, dressed in their Young Pioneer uniforms, white shirt, navy blue pants or skirt, and red string tie, singing a song about the smiling future. It reminded me of the time I recited Petöfi's poem about hanging all the kings, on Prize Day at the end of fourth grade. I really believed in that stuff—and so, judging by their uplifted faces, did the children singing that song.

WEDNESDAY, FEBRUARY 10

I took my first tramway ride this morning, from Kosztolányi Dezsö Square all the way to Deák Ferenc Square, along the ring of the inner city. A short walk away is Vörösmarty Square, a large, beautiful space—no cars allowed, stores in grand buildings on three sides, and the venerable Café Gerbeaud on the fourth. In the middle is a large statue wrapped in burlap, evidently to protect it from the weather. The square opens onto Váci Street, which is now a pedestrian mall. Lots of tourists.

From Vörösmarty Square I walked toward the river intending to find a taxi, but since none came I ended up near the Chain Bridge, on a beautiful big square with elaborate buildings facing it and yet another statue (no burlap on this one) in the middle. The square is so big and full of traffic that I didn't cross over to see whose statue it was. Instead, I crossed the bridge. It's magnificent, heavy granite and elaborate ironwork, with a superb view on both sides even though the weather was a bit hazy. Walking on the narrow passageway for pedestrians, I thought I felt some memories stirring of having crossed there as a child. But when, and with whom? Mother used to take me for walks, and so did Madame, after the war. Would we have walked this far from home? Maybe to go up to the Castle on a Sunday afternoon.

These speculations turned out to be false, because the bridge was blown up by the Germans and wasn't fully rebuilt until after we had left Budapest. A plaque at the foot tells the whole story, praising the glorious socialist workers who restored the structure to its former beauty. The inauguration ceremony took place in October 1949; by that time we were living in Vienna.

Facing the bridge on the Buda side is the *Budavár sikló,* the cable car to the Castle. It goes up at almost a ninety-degree angle, with a great rising view; the top, close to the National Gallery and the theater, is a short walk from the Collegium, where I arrived tired but happy at 3:30 P.M.

I felt elated by the beauty of the city. "It really is a great capital; it really can be compared to Paris," I told myself as the cable car rose above the river. That thought somehow makes me feel very proud, for Budapest turns out to be a city I can put next to the city I find most beautiful and seductive of all, one that has been part of my mental and emotional life during all the years when Budapest was totally outside it. Finding the link of beauty is a way to connect Budapest to my whole life, the life I spent not here, that has nothing to do with here.

FRIDAY, FEBRUARY 12

Dinner with the fellows at the Collegium this evening, very friendly. We all cooked something. I did the main

63

course—chicken paprikas, naturally. The Collegium reminds me of summer camp, with everyone far from home and eager to make new friends.

Tibor came with his wife Anna—interesting people. They left Budapest in 1956 when they were twenty and got married soon after. She's Jewish, was studying French literature before she left, and is now an anthropologist specializing in folklore. He was studying English literature and is now a sociologist. They talked about how, after more than thirty years in France, they still don't feel fully integrated, still look at things critically, like outsiders. They feel more at home in Budapest, when all's said and done. Yet, of course, they're not a hundred percent insiders here either—that good old "between" status again, I thought to myself.

SATURDAY, FEBRUARY 13

The long-awaited "other American," Robert, made his appearance among the fellows two days ago. We've hit it off well, discovered we have some things in common, including the year of our birth. He was born in San Francisco, of Hungarian Jewish parents—his father left here around 1920 and met his mother (also Hungarian) in Chicago. Robert learned Hungarian mostly in the past few years, as a way of reinforcing his European roots—we even spoke a bit, using the familiar *te*, like French *tu*. He has many contacts in Budapest, especially on the Jewish side; he feels very linked to his Jewishness. Married for twenty years, divorced ten years ago, has had numerous affairs since then. Currently he's involved with a Czech woman twenty years his junior, whom he met last summer. This time it's serious, he says. She's in the States right now on an exchange fellowship, but they talk on the phone every day.

I didn't acquire this mass of information at our first

meeting. By coincidence, we met this evening at the theater and went for a long drink afterward. Part of the "summer camp" effect is that you become intimate quickly, like strangers on a train who confide details about their lives to each other that they wouldn't reveal to people they've known for years. I told Robert about myself as well, and we compared notes about singlehood after long marriage, grown-up children and their problems (he has two daughters), and other such. One conclusion, almost too banal to state: men have it easier in the singlehood department, especially if they're perceived as powerful. Powerful men are sexy no matter what their age. With women it's just the opposite—the more powerful they are, the less sexy they're perceived to be. Just one of life's little dissymmetries. Occasionally one hears of an older, very famous woman marrying a much younger, unknown man—the Liz Taylor syndrome, still a rarity.

My sense of Robert is that he likes to be the powerful one. He's a charmer, quite attractive—but I bet he doesn't like his women to upstage him.

SUNDAY, FEBRUARY 14

Quiet morning at home. Then I went to the Collegium and wrote letters. Around 7:00 P.M. I took a taxi across the river to see a new Hungarian movie, *Roncsfilm* ("Junk Movie"), which turned out to be a cross between Monty Python and the French hit of two years ago, the gross *Delicatessen*. This one was funny and postmodernly self-conscious (people speaking directly into the camera, commenting on the events we are watching), but it got a bit tiresome because almost every episode involved a violent confrontation. In keeping with the Monty Python humor, no matter how badly people were beaten up or stabbed or burned, they reappeared in the next scene perfectly fine.

The point was to show the pent-up frustration and rage in people, always there just below the surface and ready to erupt at the slightest provocation. The opening shots show the breaking down of a wall, intercut with actual footage of the Berlin wall. But the implication is that nothing has gotten better since then. The film's subtitle is ironic: "Vagy mi van ha győztünk?" "So what if we won?" So nothing; things are still bad. The theater, incidentally, was full of young people. I was one of the very few spectators over twenty-five.

Afterward, I walked down the boulevard to the Oktogon, where the busiest place was the Burger King. I continued on Andrássy Avenue to the Opera House, very elaborate but dark (no performance tonight), and took a taxi from there. The taxi driver was extremely talkative, the first one like that I've met since I got here. He asked what kind of work I did. "I'm a *tanárnö* [teacher, which can mean anything from middle-school teacher to university professor]," I told him.

"It's a nice profession—only people with real heart can be good teachers."

"Did you go to the university?" I asked.

"Yes, I studied for five years."

"Really? What did you study?"

"Engineering. I'm an engineer."

"And now?"

"Now I drive a taxi."

Just like that, matter-of-fact. I didn't want to probe, and besides, we had arrived home.

MONDAY, FEBRUARY 15

Long lunch with Aniko today, the young scholar I met in Boston last year. She's cut her hair short, looks more glamorous and slightly "punk"—an attractive woman, and she's obviously more at home here than in the States (when she walks into a room, she expects people to look up). Yet, interestingly, she misses Cambridge. It's been almost a year since she and her husband, Peter (also an academic), got back, but she says they've been finding it hard to readjust to life in Budapest. Yes, they have tons of friends and family here, a whole support system she lacked in the States. Financially, though, life is much harsher. After ten years of university teaching and a good scholarly reputation, Peter earns 15,000 forints a month—less than $200. You can't live on that, and in fact everybody who teaches in the university has at least one other job to make ends meet. Aniko was also offered a teaching job this year, but she turned it down. She's working for a private foundation, where she earns three times as much. "I'd rather be in the library, reading, or translating an American novel," she said. But for now that's not an option.

I told her about my visit with the editor János, whom she knows. Everybody knows everybody in Budapest, it appears, at least among the intellectuals. She filled me in on János's family background—very interesting. His father was an old-style Communist, famous (or infamous) after the war: during the Stalinist period before 1956 he was the number two man for a much-feared culture commissar who "caused the ruin of many a man and woman," as Aniko put it. She thinks that János's boyish mannerisms are a reaction against his powerful father—"as if he had trouble assuming the role of a mature man, a father." Pop psychoanalysis? Maybe, but it makes sense. It's fascinating that in all the hours we spent together, he never mentioned this fact about his father. He told me only that he himself was anti-Communist—as if it made no difference that his father had been a true believer!

Budapest Diary

Dinner at the Tabáni Kakas restaurant on Attila Avenue, with Robert. Later Stani, our Polish writer, joined us and we stayed there talking until close to midnight. The restaurant lends itself to that kind of evening—it's a homey *étterem,* an "eating room" with square tables, red curtains, and a piano in the corner where a middle-aged woman plays and discreetly sings old romantic songs or folk classics like the one about blue eyes being the most beautiful. Mother loved that song; she was very proud of her blue eyes. The cuisine is mostly Jewish-style, crisp roast goose or roast duck with steamed red cabbage and hash brown potatoes, very tasty and plentiful.

Before Stani came, we spoke about personal things—family, Jewishness. Robert's girlfriend isn't Jewish, and I asked him whether that presented a problem for him. Yes, he said, but she has agreed to learn Hebrew, which he speaks fluently. In return he's learning Czech. "Besides," he added, "in Eastern Europe there are only two kinds of Christians, anti-Semites and philo-Semites, and she's a philo-Semite."

"Do you mean Jewishness is so marked in this part of the world that no indifference to it is possible?" I asked.

"That's exactly right."

"Is it different in the United States?"

"Oh yes, absolutely."

We both paused. Is it really different, back home? Yes, in most places, we decided. But I can imagine somebody arguing the opposite.

After Stani joined us we switched to French, which he speaks much better than English. He's a very lively, excitable guy with little wisps of hair, mostly balding. He has a grown son and a wife who is a journalist in Warsaw. Stani calls himself a liberal Catholic, a supporter of Lech Walesa. We spoke about politics in Poland (he's cautiously optimistic) and about "political correctness" in the United States.

To my surprise, he had never heard of "political correctness." Robert explained it in negative terms, as a "conformisme de gauche," conformity on the left. He's against all forms of "groupthink," he added, and hates intellectual pressure—for example, when students ask him why he doesn't assign any articles by blacks in his jurisprudence course. "It's not the source that matters, but the opinion; that's my firm conviction. Thurgood Marshall's opinions are great not because he was black, but because he was right."

"Yes, but many of his opinions concerned discrimination against blacks," I ventured. "And he was strongly involved in antidiscrimination issues."

"A white judge could also have handed down, and many *did* hand down, similar opinions," said Robert.

"Yes, but the fact that Thurgood Marshall was black is not totally irrelevant," said I. And so it went. Robert tried to argue that race is not a major distinguishing factor in America, but class is.

"Still, it's not by chance that the greatest proportion of blacks in the United States live in poverty," I said.

"Yes, but what do black intellectuals know about that? They're aristocrats, for heaven's sake! How can they claim to speak about the suffering of poor black people?"

"Well, an aristocrat named Moses felt he could speak about the suffering of his people."

At that he smiled: "Touché."

Later Robert and Stani ganged up on me about feminism. Stani's view, which apparently is shared by many Eastern Europeans, even some women, is that only old maids and lesbians are feminists, and that all feminists are man haters. "I hope you're not a feminist," he said to me. I tried to tell him feminism isn't exactly the bogeywoman he thinks it is: "It's a question of not assigning roles to people based exclusively on their sex or their skin color or any other biological category."

"Yes, but women should still remain women, not give up their natural qualities," he declared.

As for Robert, he wasn't much help. At one point he tried to deny that many more women were killed by their mates in the United States each year than vice versa. "Women kill too," he said, when I pointed out how many women have already been killed this year by their husbands or lovers, in Massachusetts alone. Even Stani agreed that men are more violent toward women than women are toward men. "In Poland, it's because men get drunk," he said. Finally Robert agreed too, but it was an uphill struggle.

I teased him: "Do you have a reputation as a reactionary, back home?"

"You bet I do. I hate groupthink."

"Well, we'll just have to try to convert you," I said. Reactionary or not, I like him.

TUESDAY, FEBRUARY 16

Read István Csurka's column in last week's *Magyar Forum,* which I bought yesterday. His rhetoric is clever, and so predictable that it fascinates me. This time his theme was that the good Hungarian Christian people are being silenced by "György Konrád-type liberalism"—old leftists and Communists who now call themselves liberals, but it's still the same old clique. It might seem odd that he should cite the novelist György Konrád as the model of the "old Communist," because Konrád was a well-known dissident in the old regime, often in trouble with the people in power. Now he is one of Hungary's best-known writers (his novels have been translated worldwide), and he's also an influential voice among the Free Democrats, a liberal

opposition party that disapproves of Csurka's brand of nationalism. Of course, another reason Csurka cited his
name is that Konrád is Jewish. Once again, it's those Jews
who are trying to keep us true Magyars, Christian Magyars, down. The current talk about the renewal of anti-
Semitism in Hungary is a smoke screen, according to
Csurka—what really should be talked about is the "rob-
bing of the country." In fact, this new-old clique would like
to hound the Christian Magyars not only out of politics
and public life, but out of life *tout court*: "Without persecution, there is no liberalism. They need space."

Note how he equates the current liberals and the old
Communists; and he implies, almost states outright, that
all the Communist leaders were Jews, hostile to true Magyar thought and spirit. At one point he mentions the
name of József Révai, the infamous culture commissar
János's father worked for. "Révai and his culture band, Aczél and his *shameses* jumped at the throat of the national culture," writes Csurka. He never actually uses the word
zsidó, "Jew," but *shames* (Yiddish for "sexton") is about as
explicit as you can get. A few paragraphs later he makes a
nasty dig at some of today's liberals who "sing the song of
'let's forget the past, it's no use looking backward, we have
to look forward.'" That's because, he says, some of them
"had a daddy who tore people's nails off." An allusion to
anti-Communist intellectuals like János, obviously.

I wonder who Csurka's daddy was. On the same page as
his column there's an ad for the Magyar Forum publishing
house, which has just reissued a 1938 novel about provincial life at the turn of the century, by one Péter Csurka. Any
relation to István?

Saw the second half of the documentary about the three
émigrés that started last week. This time too there was very
interesting newsreel footage from the 1950s and later. At

Stalin's death (March 1953), newsreels showed mournful workers assembled, then marching in silent funeral parades. They showed other mass marches and demonstrations as well, with enormous portraits of Stalin and Rákosi floating above the crowd. As late as 1985, one party speaker (was it János Kádár? I didn't recognize him), discussing Hungarian politics at what looked like a dinner meeting, stated that experience in Hungary has shown a one-party system is best. "There is nothing wrong in principle with a multiparty system," he said, "but Hungarian history shows that in this country it hasn't worked."

The only reply to that, I guess, is Scarlett's "Tomorrow is another day."

WEDNESDAY, FEBRUARY 17

It snowed today, leaving a light dusting on the sidewalks. I had another very long visit, this time with Eva, who teaches French literature at the university and has two other academic jobs as well. I met her at the Institute of Literary Studies, where she's a researcher. She's about my age, plumpish, attractive, with a friendly smile—she immediately asked if we could use the familiar *te*, so much less complicated. I gather women use *te* with each other more easily than with a man, and the same is true of men. It would never have occurred to János to say *te* to me, even after our four-hour meeting.

Eva and I chatted awhile over coffee, then she took me up to look at the library, which has precious nineteenth-century periodicals among its treasures. Eva introduced me to the librarian and got permission for me to borrow books. I immediately borrowed *The Oxford History of Hungarian Literature* by Loránt Czigány, which she recommended. I've already read big chunks of it.

After the library we went back to her office and talked

for another hour, this time in French. I still don't feel I can conduct a serious conversation in Hungarian; I wonder when that will change. (Will it change?) She asked if I'd be willing to give a lecture or seminar at the Institute. "With pleasure. I'll talk about feminism, just to be provocative," I said. She laughed, finding the idea quite attractive. Earlier we had spoken about feminist criticism, and she confirmed my sense that people here know very little about it. But she added that right now, with so many bigger problems that also affect men, she'd rather not dwell on women's problems or pit women against men. This sounded like the Marxist-feminist thesis in France during the 1970s ("First the revolution, then women's problems"), and I didn't want to get into an argument about it. I remarked that not all feminist criticism is directed against men. She wasn't fully convinced, however.

We spoke at length about Csurka. Péter Csurka, as I suspected, was his father and was also a right-winger, a journalist and novelist. Eva said Csurka wrote some very good plays during the "ancien régime" ("Alas," she added), and no one could tell from them he was an anti-Semite. In fact he and György Konrád considered themselves on the same side. "You have to understand, that was in the good old days when we were all together in opposing the regime. Our opposition was so strong that none of us realized our differences. Only afterward did we split into two hostile camps."

"But didn't anyone notice his anti-Semitism?"

"No! Oh, there were stories occasionally, about how he got drunk at some party with other writers and started to 'Jew'—*zsidózni*; you see we even have a verb for it. But otherwise he kept it under wraps. Maybe if we went back and reread his plays now we'd find signs." He also wrote some good stories, she said. He's about sixty, like Konrád. Very interesting, this story of brothers in arms who find themselves, before long, deadly enemies.

The Czigány literary history is fascinating and makes many things come to life, including the place-names of Budapest. Vörösmarty Square, so central, is named after Mihály Vörösmarty, a nineteenth-century poet, the first of the great poets after the language reform of the early years of the century. Kazinczy Street, which I had always associated with Jewishness—no doubt because of the Orthodox synagogue there—is named after a Catholic, Ferenc Kazinczy, a minor nobleman who was one of the architects of the language reform. (The reform involved, mainly, standardizing spelling and expanding the vocabulary so that abstract concepts and technical terms would no longer have to be borrowed from Latin or German.) To an American, it's astonishing how many streets and squares and institutions are named after writers and intellectuals: Attila József (great modernist poet), Dezsö Kosztolányi (writer associated with the important review *Nyugat, West*, from the early years of this century), János Arany (nineteenth-century lyric poet), Imre Madách (author of the epic drama *The Tragedy of Man*), Frigyes Karinthy (another *Nyugat* writer, good friend of Kosztolányi), Mór Jókai (nineteenth-century novelist), and many, many others, including of course the hero Sándor Petöfi, forever associated with the 1848 revolution. Petöfi is like Victor Hugo in France—every city, large or small, has at least one street or square named after him.

I kept thinking about Mother this evening, especially when I spread out the map of Hungary to look for Nyíregyháza, the city where she was born, after reading the *History*. (Another great turn-of-the century writer, Gyula Krudy, was from Nyíregyháza.) What a pity she's not alive now, for her and for me! I would so much have loved to ask her about her childhood and about some of the small towns she knew. A few names in the same region sound familiar. I want to find Mother's birth certificate, though I couldn't say exactly why.

THURSDAY, FEBRUARY 18

Exhausted. I must have walked miles today, all around my old neighborhood. Tramway to Deák Square, then up Király Street to the yellow church, then right on Acacia Street. Király Street has beautiful turn-of-the-century buildings, elaborately decorated. Some look in bad shape, others look redone, and it's the same in that whole neighborhood. Visually, it's a grab bag: some decrepit shops and some newfangled ones selling computers, electronics, Italian shoes. Acacia Street is mostly decrepit, at least the part I walked on. The first two houses on the odd-numbered side are black with soot and practically crumbling, though once they must have been grand, with ornate columns and carvings. Then comes a long, low building I didn't remember at all, and after that, number 59. The Foto Optika store I found so ugly in 1984 when I went with the boys is still there, though this time it didn't bother me as much. I don't think I noticed, last time, that there are statues decorating the curved top of the facade. The three balconies, including our old one on the top left, look as if they're ready to fall down.

I went into the courtyard, very oblong indeed, then into the stairwell. The wrought iron railings are still there, still beautiful. An elderly woman dressed in red was crossing the courtyard when I walked in, and she looked at me curiously. I felt odd, like an intruder. No question of going up to the third floor and knocking on the old apartment door again, though I may do it one of these days—maybe if someone else is with me. Meanwhile, standing at the bottom of the stairwell, I remembered the time after Daddy's heart attack when he had to be carried up the stairs every day, since there was no elevator and he was forbidden to climb. He had hired two men who would come and join hands to form a seat, on which he sat with an arm around each man's neck. This continued until we left the country, or until we moved out to the summer house, where he didn't have to worry about stairs. That was around June 1949.

He had had the operation for his ulcer in March, then the heart attack a few days later, followed by the long recovery, first in the hospital and then at home. It must have been in May or early June that he gave the "thanksgiving" dinner for all the Talmudic scholars of which I have a photograph at home: a large table full of men dressed in black caftans and black hats, with Daddy about the only one wearing a regular suit and hat. He wrote a learned speech for the occasion, a textual commentary he practiced for weeks beforehand while I listened. It was in Yiddish, so I didn't understand a word, but every time he said the word "Rambam" I would go into gales of laughter—for some mysterious reason, that inner rhyme struck me as hilarious. After a while it became a whole production; I would laugh even though I no longer found it funny, because I thought he expected me to. What did it matter that Rambam was Maimonides, a great scholar of the Middle Ages? All I cared about was that Daddy should find me rapt and charming.

Coming out into the street again, I noticed that the building directly across, number 60, had been knocked down—they seem to be getting ready to build a new house there. I crossed the street and stared intently at the facade again. A little girl walking home from school went by and turned around to look at me. I felt too self-conscious to take out my camera again (I had photographed the statues on the facade before going into the courtyard), as if people would notice and not like it. I noticed, or maybe only imagined, that a man standing in front of the building was staring at me suspiciously: What was I doing there, inspecting the place so closely? I suddenly felt tired and hungry, and besides, I had had enough nostalgia for one day.

The "Evening with Miklós Vajda," sponsored by the journal *2000*, turned out to be fascinating. Vajda, a well-known editor and translator, was a teenager during the war, son of a Greek Orthodox mother and converted Jewish father. He said he thought of the war, including the last terrible year, as an "adventure" (*kaland*). The *2000* editor who was doing the interviewing remarked that last month's guest, George Soros (the well-known financier), had used the same word, and I thought of what I say about adventure in my own piece on the war. It must be due to our having been so privileged before, so loved and surrounded by adoring relatives, we thought we were invincible. That, at least, is how Vajda explained it. His parents had some powerful friends, including a famous actress who was his godmother. In my more modest way, I too was a totally spoiled and adored child who took all the adulation as her due. One more piece of luck, perhaps.

The other thing worth noting about the "Evening" is that it lasted almost three hours! Scheduled to start at 7:00 P.M., it actually started at 7:20, with about a hundred people in the audience. The two men sat on the stage with microphones and talked—or rather, Vajda talked about his life with a few well-placed interventions and questions from the editor. At 8:40 the editor announced we would take a break, just as I thought the evening was going to end. The break lasted twenty minutes, then we were back for another hour. The audience sat patiently on the uncomfortable chairs, listening intently. Vajda said at one point: "To be here in the darkest period of the Rákosi era [from about

77

1949 to 1953], one could survive only by laughing a lot." He and his friends laughed a lot, but it wasn't all a laughing matter. His mother spent several months in jail for being a "class enemy" and left the country in 1956. He had been scheduled to leave several years earlier and even made it as far as Italy. But he changed his mind and came back: he was too attached to the Hungarian language and Hungarian literature, he discovered, to leave them behind.

Around 9:55, the editor asked the audience if they had questions. I had been reflecting for close to an hour that this kind of duologue could never happen back home, where questions from the audience would have taken up at least half the time. Here there were only two questions—as if one could get a discussion going with an audience that had sat through almost three hours of its own silence.

I feel very lucky to be able to attend events like this and understand what's being said. My abstract Hungarian vocabulary is growing by leaps and bounds—now I even know the word for "concept"!

FRIDAY, FEBRUARY 19

This morning I finally got to the Gellért baths. It was about 9:30, and not too many women were there yet, so I had only a half-hour wait for my massage. In the meantime I went into the common hot pool, the thermal bath. What a place! When we first go in and get our cabana, we're given a funny little apron, which most people don't wear. I tried mine on in the dressing room—it's made of white, slightly yellowed cotton, and covers approximately one-third of the front of the body. In the back there's only the string. This is a truly odd piece of apparel to wear into a pool, or anywhere else. Its function is evidently to hide the belly and pubic area as well as a bit of the breasts. But since it leaves all of the backside uncovered, it looks more like something out of a Victorian porn novel than a modest cover-up.

Carrying my apron, I went down the stairs, passing a number of women of various shapes and ages who were also promenading naked. A few actually had their aprons on and looked quite strange. After taking an obligatory shower I entered the baths, which consist of two symmetrical pools on each side of a central walkway. They are in a tall, mosaic-lined hall with a glass ceiling, from which all sounds reverberate in deep echoes. Thus there is a constant chattering in the baths, like birds singing, even though relatively few women are actually talking to each other. This chattering sound is the accompanying music to our ablutions.

There are women here of every shape, size, and age. Most are wearing caps; some are doing exercises in the water, moving their necks or throwing their arms out to the sides or even jumping up and down. A few are slowly swimming from one side of the pool to the other (there's a sign on the wall saying it's forbidden to make noise or to swim around, but no one pays attention to that). One or two women are sitting directly under the taps from which the water flows in thin streams, turning their bodies so the water hits them in different places. At one point two women who look like mother and daughter, perhaps fifty-five and thirty, enter the pool. I notice how firm the younger woman's body looks, compared with the sagging outline of the older one. In some cases, however, there's an interesting contrast between the face and the body, like the woman in a swimming cap whose face is that of a sixty-year-old or more but whose breasts are high and firm like a thirty-year-old's. The rest of her body is not so young, even though she's slender; telltale sags around the back of the thighs and hips announce that this is an older woman's body.

There are some really old women, with big rolls of fat and breasts that hang down to their knees (or so it seems). And in between an astonishing variety: round breasts and flat breasts, big breasts and small breasts, high breasts and low breasts. It is rare to see a truly beautiful body, with well-defined breasts, a nicely indented waist, and curvy but not oversize hips. I compare mine with the other women's and decide it's not among the worst. There's too much fat around the belly, but I have a waist and my hips are passable—as for the legs, they're grade A (OK, OK—sheer vanity).

I swam around for a while, watching the clock. After twenty minutes in the bath, I was beginning to sweat. The water is 38° Celsius, close to 100° Fahrenheit, yet it doesn't feel too hot. I went out to see about the massage line, and after a few minutes it was my turn. Three masseuses work in a single room. The floor is very wet, because this is the "with water" massage, which means they use soap and water instead of oils. Every once in a while the masseuse washes you down with a hose, then directs the hose over the floor to wash away the soap.

The three customers, including me, were getting our bodies worked over like pieces of meat while the masseuses talked and joked with each other or occasionally talked to us. "Where is the lady from?" mine asked me after a while.

"From Boston, from America," I answered. She was about forty, with a tired, kind face and her hair in a topknot, dressed in what is apparently the masseuses' uniform, short white cotton trousers and a white T-shirt, much of it wet. I asked how she knew I was from elsewhere: From my accent? She smiled and nodded. After I went upstairs and got dressed, I went back and slipped a bill into her hand. She thanked me and said, "I'm Mari. Next time you come, ask for me. You won't have to wait in line."

Through a Stranger's Eyes

Later, in the Collegium, I bumped into the rector in the hall: always bouncy, with a huge smile on his face, he looks as if he enjoyed life tremendously. "Hello, Zsuzsa!" he boomed—with him I speak only Hungarian; he gets a kick out of it, and for some reason I'm not embarrassed, even when I have to stammer for a word. He told me he had just seen our colleague Farkas, a well-known economist I met in Cambridge a few months ago. "I told him I thought you were having a good time," the rector said, laughing. I went over to Farkas's office to say hello and found him already set up for work, secretary and all—he just got back from his American semester last week. Tall, slightly stooped, soft-spoken and slow moving, he forms an interesting contrast to the rector's mercurial figure. Like Prospero and Ariel in *The Tempest*. His face lit up with a warm smile when he saw me. After a few minutes he said: "Your Hungarian is much better than the last time we talked. It's extraordinary!" That made me feel very proud, as if I'd gotten a good grade in school.

In the taxi home this evening, the driver asked where I was from: "You speak Hungarian, but I can tell you haven't lived here."

"I'm from America."

"Your parents are Hungarian?"

"Yes, and I was born here too. But I left when I was ten."

"In 1956?"

"Yes, around then." (Chalk up a point for looking younger than you are.) Then we started to talk about the current economic situation. Many Americans are coming here to set up businesses, he said: "They're optimistic." As for him, he thinks things will get better, but not for a while.

"Provided there isn't some kind of civil war in the meantime," he said darkly.

"Civil war? What do you mean?"

"Oh, the Csurka band."

"Do you think Csurka's attracting a lot of people?" I asked, intrigued.

"Not at the moment, but if things get worse he might—people who have nothing to lose. If the unemployment doesn't improve, for example. There are one million people out of work, out of a total of four to five million."

"What? 25 percent unemployment?"

"Yes, 20 to 25 percent of the active population; the others are too old."

"That's serious." I asked whether he expected some changes after next year's elections.

"In a real democracy, the government would've fallen by now, but these guys will do anything to stay in power. They'll even falsify the election results."

"And who will you vote for?"

"Not the MDF, that's for sure!"

Now there was a lesson in political economy. The actual unemployment figures, according to Farkas, are less drastic than my taxi driver thinks: 13.3 percent, no worse than the rest of Europe. But it looks terrible, Farkas explained, because before 1989 unemployment was zero. Productivity was low, but everybody had a job. Now it has all changed, and people aren't used to it. They were expecting only the virtues, not the vices, of capitalism.

As for civil war, the taxi driver appears to exaggerate Csurka's influence. But it's true that the MDF is not as popular as it was in 1990, when its talk about "traditional Hungarian values" could be seen as a welcome change from Communism. Today there are other, more liberal anti-Communist parties to choose among.

SATURDAY, FEBRUARY 20

Party at a journalist's apartment, a huge place across from the American embassy. There must have been hundreds of people there—writers, academics, liberal politicians, plus a large contingent of foreign visitors. I saw the American poet Stephen, who's here on a Fulbright exchange, and my friend Aniko, looking beautifully provocative, with heavily rouged cheeks and spiky hair. Stephen introduced me to an interesting woman, Julie, a journalist from Toronto whose life story resembles mine except that she's a few years younger—she left in 1956 after three years of elementary school. Her Hungarian is pretty good, somewhat like mine in that she doesn't know many abstract words. She's here for a few weeks, to teach a journalism course at the university.

Julie told me that one of the men there had published a moving essay in a Canadian journal last year, about how he discovered he was Jewish. Another Hungarian "of Jewish origin": *Zsidó származású*; I've heard or read that expression half a dozen times since I've been here. Few are ready to affirm simply "I am a Jew." But to be "of Jewish origin" is admissible.

SUNDAY, FEBRUARY 21

I bought some carnations at a stand on the way to the tram stop this afternoon, to put in the vase on my desk. As the young man was wrapping them, I noticed bunches of snowdrops, dozens of them on their stalks in a shallow pan. These flowers are smaller than the ones we have in America, so you need many of them to make a tiny bouquet. It must be a huge amount of work to make dozens of bunches, each one wrapped in a green leaf and tied with string. I wasn't sure of the flower's name, so I asked the vendor. Until then I think he took me for a Hungarian, but my question obviously told him I wasn't. *Hóvirág*, he said, looking at me curiously. Snowflower. I took a bunch out of the pan and gave it to him to wrap.

"Are you from England?" he asked.

"No, from America." After that, he spoke to me only in English.

Hóvirág. Small white bouquets wrapped in green leaves, beckoning at the flower stands. Evening on the boulevard; the shops are still open when darkness falls. I stop with Madame and we buy a bunch of hóvirág, *snowflowers for the end of winter. A few weeks later it will be* ibolya, *violets nestled against velvety leaves—I bury my face in them, inhale the sweet smell. How I love the coming of spring!*

Neither a foreigner nor a Hungarian, but something in between. Just a little off-center, not quite the real thing, though sometimes close to passing for it. One could make this into a sign of unhappiness, or on the contrary a sign of uniqueness, of special status. Except that there are whole armies of people like me, not unique, unless it's a collective uniqueness. Is that what we call history?

Most of the current issue of *Magyar Forum* is devoted to the founding meeting of the Magyar Út movement, the Hungarian Way. István Csurka got to be on page 1 in a large photo showing him on the platform at the meeting, page 2 with his weekly column, and pages 3–4, which carried the complete text of his speech. There is a close-up of him on the podium, a thick, blunt-faced man with receding hairline and double chin. "His name should be Csunya," I say to myself while studying the photo. (*Csunya* means ugly—how nasty of me!) He wears tinted glasses, looks a bit like the French right-wing leader Jean-Marie Le Pen. Why do all these demagogues resemble beefy parodies of "real men," the kind that would never in a million years eat quiche?

The page 2 column is about the ministerial shakeup of

last week. Mr. Csurka is not happy that his party, the MDF, is contemplating a move toward the center, squeezing out the "national radicals" whose leader he is. National radicals—the phrase comes up at least four times—sounds ominously like National Socialists to me. The usual theme: the people, the *nép*, are being kept down by the *nomenklatura*, who used to be Communists but are now liberals.

And the speech? More of the same. True Hungarians have "Hungarianness" (*Magyarság*), a matter of blood. They're descendants of Árpád. Christians. What all true Hungarians detest is "Naphta-liberalism," and here Csurka the onetime playwright and short-story writer opens a parenthesis to explain about Naphta. Thomas Mann, he tells us, modeled this character in *The Magic Mountain* on the philosopher György Lukács, who "as everyone knows liked to vacation in Swiss resorts" during the years before "he threw his lot in with the terror and with the Hungarian Red soldiers"—that's an allusion to the short-lived Communist government of 1919 led by Béla Kun, in which Lukács acted as culture commissar. And of course everyone also knows that Lukács was Jewish, or rather "of Jewish origin," as were all the other members of the Kun government. Liberals *equal* Communists *equal* Jews, the tried-and-true formula. But Csurka says the Magyar Út is neither right nor left, just Hungarian.

The joke is that in *The Magic Mountain,* the philosopher Naphta is not a liberal at all, but a Nietzschean pessimist who often expresses views we would associate with fascism. Such fine distinctions don't appear to bother Mr. Csurka, however.

TUESDAY, FEBRUARY 23

A disturbing thing happened this afternoon. I went to the post office near the Collegium, and afterward to the local small supermarket. As I was crossing the narrow vestibule between the outer entrance and the inner door, I felt a pull on my shoulder bag, but I didn't really notice it until I had entered the store. Then I did—the bag was open, my wallet gone. Pickpocketed? But it was impossible; it had happened too fast! Behind me four teenage boys walked in, and I thought to myself: "They must have done it!" But I couldn't figure out exactly what had happened, and besides, the boys didn't look like hoodlums. Still, my wallet was missing.

At that point I looked down. Surprise! The wallet lay on the floor. I picked it up. It was dusty but otherwise untouched—the few bills were still in it. Very likely the boys had taken it then thrown it away, maybe because they saw me turn around just as they walked in and got scared, or because there wasn't enough money in the wallet to interest them, or because they'd decided to be nice.

Everyone says crime is on the increase in the city—another legacy of "the Change." Yet I generally feel safer walking alone at night here than in many American cities. Today's incident has made me wary. It's not a good idea to walk down the deserted road in back of the Castle by myself at night. On Sunday night I walked down that road and then took a long, dark set of stairs to the street. Foolhardy.

In 1951 or 1952, when I was about twelve, I walked through Central Park by myself one December evening. I was on my way home from a doctor's appointment, heading east in the Eighty-sixth Street crosstown bus. The park looked so beautiful in the snow I wanted to walk through it, and I got off the bus. It was early evening, already dark. I saw a few people in the distance—otherwise I was alone. I knew I was doing something daring and felt strangely pleased with myself. The soft snow fell on my hair and eyelids; I arrived home covered with it, happy. I didn't tell Mother what I had done.

Through a Stranger's Eyes

I've often thought back on that night, how innocently foolhardy I was, and how lucky. In later years I remember one or two other adventures of this kind, where I took unnecessary risks with physical danger. It occurs to me those acts may have been aftertraces of the war adventure and the adventure of leaving Hungary, as if I needed every once in a while to relive the excitement of life-and-death danger, and especially of overcoming it—for despite the danger, I had survived, hadn't I? The presence of snow and darkness in several of my later adventures suddenly strikes me as significant. Snow played a big role in the winter of 1945, when we would gather it at night and melt it to make water.

These days I may be testing my age as well. Am I still capable of doing the things, including risky, foolhardy things, I did when I was young? I think of my friend Shirley's saying to me in Princeton last month, when we were talking about the end of her therapy and her sorrow at leaving her therapist: "I'm going to miss him a lot, but in a way that's exactly what this therapy has been about—realizing that with age, you're called on more and more to bid good-bye to things that matter to you." A wise thought, but I hate it. I'd rather quote Dylan Thomas: "Rage, rage against the dying of the light." Am I going to become one of those intrepid, ridiculous old ladies who go on safaris at age ninety? Why not?

This weekend's *Magyar Nemzet* ("Hungarian Nation," a centrist newspaper) had a very interesting article about the trial and execution of László Rajk, in 1949. Rajk was a hard-line Communist throughout the 1930s, one of Rákosi's old buddies who fought in the Spanish civil war, and he had an important post in the government until he was arrested. He was hanged on trumped-up charges, not an untypical case for that time: the revolution eating its own children, as in the Soviet Union in the 1930s. A team of historians is currently editing documents for a "history of the administration of justice," and their most recent volume deals with the Rajk case. The newspaper published the original document recounting the accusations against Rajk. Fascinating stuff: the accusation tells the story of Rajk's activities in the 1930s as if he had been a double agent, working for the secret police during all that time. The main outlines of the story remain unchanged (they can't deny he was in Spain, for example), but its meaning is completely transformed because the story attributes intentions to him that put a negative light on everything he did. Thus, when he went to agitate for the Party in Czechoslovakia in the early 1930s, "it was the secret police who sent him"; when he went to Spain to fight, it was with "specific instructions to sow confusion and defeat in the ranks." No doubt about it: everything depends on who's telling the story, and for what purpose.

We left Hungary just before Rajk's trial in September 1949. Could that have been one of the catalysts for the decision to leave? Probably not. The whole thing was too much a settling of scores among Communists to have an effect on ordinary people like us. More likely the arrest of my aunt Rózsi and her husband János Czinner as "class enemies" the previous February had a much stronger impact. They were kept in jail for several weeks, and their lumberyard was nationalized. My aunt Rózsi remembers a newspaper somebody showed her in jail, with a big headline: "How They Sawed off Czinner the Lumber King." She told me that Mother, trying to visit them one day, happened to see János being escorted from the prison to a hearing room on the next street, handcuffed and with a chain on his legs. He was a big, strong man and must have looked frightening. A woman on the street said to Mother: "He probably murdered somebody." She was too scared, or shocked by the sight, to reply. A few months after their release, the Czinners were allowed to leave the country—minus most of their possessions, naturally.

WEDNESDAY, FEBRUARY 24

Saw the operetta *János Vitéz,* based on Petöfi's poem, at the theater tonight. There were about three hundred children there! They looked like they were on class excursions, third- or-fourth graders—just the age I was when we left. The operetta has some lovely music and a few comic moments too. "A cross between Ferenc Lehár and Gilbert and Sullivan," I whispered to Robert, who came with me.

The story is about fidelity in love, but even more about fidelity to the native land. The hero, whose name used to be Johnny Corn but who becomes Sir John (János Vitéz), is offered half of France and the king's beautiful daughter after he saves them from the Turks, but he remains faithful to his blond Iluska and to the village on the *puszta* where he grew up. In the end, even Iluska has to take second place to the hometown: when he finds her in Fairyland after she has died, she expects him to stay there with her forever—but just as he's about to drink the cup of forgetfulness, he hears the melody he used to play on his shepherd's pipe and realizes he must go home. "If you love me, you'll follow me," he tells her. And she does. The big red–white-and-green Hungarian flag is waved twice in the play, with a great flourish. *Honvágy,* longing for the native land, is probably the strongest emotion expressed.

The music sounded familiar, but the only song I actually recognized was "Kék tó, tiszta tó," in which János begs the Lake of Life to give him back his beloved Iluska, just before throwing in the red rose from her grave. I'm certain I saw the play as a child, though I have no idea exactly when or how. Maybe with my class, like the children tonight, or maybe Mother took me.

Budapest Diary

"Boy, if I had seen this as a child, I'd be crying buckets of nostalgia right now," Robert said at the end, when I told him I remembered the "blue lake, pure lake" song. "Or else," he added, "I'd rush home to write about it."

Is it nostalgia I feel, remembering that song? I don't think so, at least not more than any adult reexperiencing an event lived in childhood. But I'm beginning to feel a strong curiosity about what my life would have been like had we not left. Julie, the Canadian journalist I met at the party the other night, said something similar: "Everytime I walk down the street, it's as if my doppelgänger were walking behind me."

Who is my doppelgänger?

I love Stalin. *Sometimes, before falling asleep, I ask myself with a tight throat, "What would happen if Stalin died? Who would protect us then?" Protect us from Hitler, or from the dreaded Nyilas with their leather boots and guns? Just protect us.*

I am an ardent Pioneer, *wearing my uniform with pride and reciting inflammatory poems against royalty on Prize Day. Later I belong to the Party Youth and am among those marching in silence, tears streaming down my face, the day Stalin dies. When 1956 comes around, I'm not among the rioting students, pulling down Stalin's statue. I'm in my last year of gymnasium, studying for my entrance exams to the university. I want to be a doctor, like my uncle Luli in Bratislava, who was a partisan, a freedom fighter, during the war. When I am denied entrance because of my bourgeois background and suspect family (the Czinner couple, arrested in 1949, are still remembered in high places), my faith wavers, but only for a moment. The following year, I am admitted.*

I am an ardent Pioneer. *In 1953, at one of the Party Youth meetings, I meet my first love, a philosophy student at the university: Csaba. Not Jewish, and not much of a Party member either.*

Through a Stranger's Eyes

*Csaba's friends are sardonic, brilliant, and increasingly critical of
the regime. The more time I spend with them, the less I believe in
the Party or in Stalin, who in any case is dead. When 1956 comes
around, Csaba is among the leaders of the insurrection, and I am
by his side. Mother tries to keep me from going out, but she really
can't stop me, and Daddy is an invalid. After Csaba is killed, I
lose the desire to live. I do crazy things, take wild risks, but by
some miracle am never caught. I even graduate from the gymnasium on time and go on to the university to study philosophy.
There I meet Gyuri, my husband, and drop out after two years
when my first child is born. I later go back to get my degree and
become a schoolteacher.*

I am an ardent Pioneer. *In 1956, after Daddy dies of his second
heart attack, Mother and I leave the country—I don't want to, but
she insists and I can't let her go alone. In New York I meet another Hungarian refugee student and we get married. My husband and I still have many friends in Budapest—it's the only place
we really feel at home.*

Plausible possibilities all. But I don't know enough, con-
cretely, about what it was like to live here as a young adult
between 1949 and 1956, or even later. The film I saw yesterday—Péter Gothár's *Megáll az idö, Time Stands Still*—gave a
beautiful portrait of 1960s adolescents whose parents had
been among the rebels of 1956; but neither of those is exactly my generation. I'm between the two.

THURSDAY, FEBRUARY 25

Theater, saw a dramatic adaptation of my childhood favorite, *The Boys from Paul Stret.* All the boys' roles were played
by young women, which at first was strange, but after a
while one forgot about it. The theater was full of children,
but this time there were a lot of grown-ups as well. I went

with Julie, my new Canadian Hungarian friend. She too loved that novel as a child, just one of our many common experiences. During intermission we heard a cute boy, about ten or eleven, say to his teacher: "This is more like *The Girls from Paul Street*." She told him to stop acting like a smart aleck.

It was a wonderful production, lovingly evoking the customs and costumes of turn-of-the-century schoolboys. And would you believe it, I actually cried at the death of Nemecsek! So did Julie. Afterward we went for dinner at a restaurant on Acacia Street; the houses there are even more decrepit than on my block, a real slum. But the restaurant is charming, very popular with the intellectual crowd (not that we recognized anybody), and serves good home cooking. I enjoyed exchanging life stories with Julie. Her family emigrated to Vancouver in 1956, and she went to the university there. She's been married to the same man for more than twenty years, also a journalist. They have two children, a grown-up girl and a much younger boy. Julie is short and slender, with dark hair and a vivacious smile. She speaks English perfectly, but if you really listen for it, you hear the very slight trace of a Hungarian accent. Just like me. I had an intuition, when I met her at that party, that we would become friends. Tonight confirmed it.

At dinner we talked about our feelings toward Hungary. Do we feel Hungarian? Yes, but that statement must always be qualified if one is a Jew. Julie's great-uncle, who's ninety-three, tells her stories about how hard it was for him to become a doctor in Hungary around 1920. After the Kun regime fell, in 1919, there was so much anti-Jewish sentiment in the country that Jews were excluded from the university altogether, and he had to study in Prague. After a while he was expelled from there too, and when he came back he had to submit detailed documents showing how long his family had been settled in Hungary in order to be allowed to attend the university.

"We don't realize how unusual we are, in North America, where one can become a Canadian or an American citizen by choice and be considered full-fledged," Julie said. "None of the 'blood and earth' stuff one is constantly hearing about in Europe." Yes, the hyphenated American is not a bad thing. According to some people (like that true Magyar István Csurka, who I understand is actually from Slovakia), a "Hungarian Jew," let alone a "Chinese Hungarian," is a contradiction in terms.

Who needs Hungary?

SUNDAY, FEBRUARY 28

Friday night, dinner at Hanna's kosher restaurant with Robert. A big, noisy room above the courtyard of the Kazinczy Street synagogue—where my school used to be. I couldn't see the building well tonight since it was dark, but Robert said it had been renovated. Even the synagogue, which was boarded up nine years ago, is being used now, though not in winter because it's too cold. There are about twenty synagogues in Budapest, someone at our table told us. Budapest has one of the largest Jewish communities in Eastern Europe at present (about 70,000 people) and is the only place in the region with a rabbinical seminary.

There were two tables of Chasidic men and boys in the restaurant; they made a lot of noise singing, as did a large table of students from the local religious school. After a while it became deafening, and I wished they would stop. At our table, besides Robert and me and a few people whose names I didn't catch, there was a young American couple, Mark and his girlfriend Emily, who were acquaintances of Robert's, and another American named Sandy, with his German girlfriend. Sandy, an individual of uncertain occupation—"He made money in real estate and now plays the marimba," Mark said by way of introduction—looked friendly, with open face and black curly hair. But he and I got into a heated argument over Orthodox Jewry: he claimed that only the strictly Orthodox wing of Judaism is authentically Jewish, and that Conservative Jews were like criminals because they took it upon themselves to "break the contract with God unilaterally" instead of relying on the "Supreme Court Judges," the Orthodox rabbis.

His legalistic analogies really irked me, and I kept feeding the flame by rebutting his arguments. Finally I said, "Listen, we're not in a theocracy, so your legalistic comparisons don't hold. And am I ever glad! I would never live in a theocracy."

Playing his trump card, he asked, "Do you believe in God?"

"No," I replied, and that finally shut him up.

Afterward Robert said, "But you did egg him on, you know."

"Well, it reminded me of the arguments I used to have with my father, about Jews who observed the Law of the Sabbath but cheated their customers. I claimed they weren't good Jews; he claimed I didn't know what I was talking about."

"That's why you were so involved," Robert said. And I realized he was right. All those passionate arguments I had with Daddy about what it meant to be an ethical human being! I could never win, never bring him around to my point of view. But I didn't understand then what it means to be a true believer. For him, the religious man's relation to God, prescribed by minute observances, existed in a realm apart; and it was paramount. Of course he didn't condone dishonesty in everyday life, but he considered it not comparable. This way of thinking is entirely foreign to me. I wonder whether, if he had lived longer, we would have drifted apart, become truly strangers to each other.

After leaving the restaurant (I had a serious headache by then), we wound up with Mark and Emily at the latest "in" jazz club, Picasso's Points, near the Nyugati train station. Various people drifted in and greeted Mark, who seems to have a whole circle of acquaintances in Budapest. One of them, a tall, youngish Hungarian, was introduced as a poet but told me he was a diplomat. I asked him whether I could "pass" for a native Hungarian or whether he could tell I didn't live here the moment I opened my mouth.

"Yes, I can tell," he said.

"Why?"

"It's your intonation. Hungarian is a monotonous language, with stress always placed on the first syllable. Your words are more singsong."

So much for the idea that I sound native, that it's only my small vocabulary that reveals my foreignness! He consoled me: "You do sound native, but it's obvious you haven't lived here for a long time."

I think my Hungarian varies a lot—sometimes I sound like a foreigner, and at other times I could pass, linguistically if not in terms of clothes or demeanor. But why should it matter to me whether I pass or not? Is it because not passing is an indication that I don't completely fit anywhere, not even in my native city?

The Center of Europe

I left Boston one month ago. My friends in America have shrunk to the size of figures on the horizon, waving in the sunset to a departing boat. Probably as the time draws near for my return they'll get bigger. I wonder whether this is part of my "immigrant mentality," leaving the past behind as if it were gone forever. Why did I think for so many years that *The Boys from Paul Street* was just a fragment of my childhood, gone? Generations of schoolchildren have continued to read it since I left Hungary. But for me, finding it again in 1984 was like a miracle.

Maybe it has to do with trust. I don't always trust enough in the persistence of things, people, feelings—as if once I'm not there, they'll disappear.

Julie is looking into obtaining Hungarian citizenship in addition to her Canadian one. She figures that if Hungary ever becomes part of the Common Market, citizenship will entitle her and her children to work anywhere in Europe. What a thought—to be a Hungarian again! The first step is to find her birth certificate, in the district where she was registered. After she gets the document, it has to be certified and delivered to a Hungarian consulate in Canada. Of course I could never be a "real" Hungarian. But am I a real American?

WEDNESDAY, MARCH 3

We had our first fellows' seminar at the Collegium this afternoon. Stani led the discussion, on the subject of "Central Europe." We started with an essay by Czeslaw Milosz, in which Milosz says two attitudes are typical of Central

The Center of Europe

European intellectuals: a heavy sense of history and a strong sense of irony. Stani added a few more, including fatalism, hopelessness ("What good is it to work when it all comes to nothing?"), and dependency. He suggested it's because of the desire to prove they can stand on their own, without depending on anyone else, that Central European nations are so unwilling to federate and seek instead to assert their independence even if it means breaking up a previous federation—as in Czechoslovakia or, much worse, Yugoslavia.

We had a lengthy discussion, chiefly around the question whether "Central Europe" really exists as such. Stani had proposed "Western Europe" and "the rest of Europe"; Tibor, by contrast, proposed not only Central Europe, but an east versus west division within that. Poland, Hungary, and the Czech part of former Czechoslovakia are the "western" parts, while Romania, Ukraine, and Slovakia are "eastern." For him those are loaded terms: the West represents modernization, a push for political independence, and in general all that's admirable; the East represents a kind of barbarism, though he didn't use that word.

Robert said he doubted there was such a thing as Central Europe, given that few people identify themselves as "Central Europeans." Eva, my friend from the Institute of Literary Studies (I had invited her to join us), responded that she never feels anything but Hungarian in Hungary but feels Central European when she goes to Prague and recognizes the same yellow churches, the same faces, or to Paris, where she immediately spots the visiting Poles, Czechs, Romanians—the poor relations to the French. Stani said he much prefers recognizing difference to claiming sameness—which is fine, I said, as long as the differences aren't turned into reasons for massacre. Finally we all decided it was time to go for dinner at the Tabáni Kakas.

At dinner I sat next to Sanda, the art historian fellow from

97

Bucharest. She's an intense-looking, quiet woman, about my age, whose face is completely transformed when she smiles (which isn't often). I like talking with her; she has a very direct way of approaching just about any subject. Her English is a bit halting, but she knows it well and speaks it with a Romanian accent that's quite different from the Hungarian one. We often speak French, though, because she feels more comfortable in it. Tonight she told me a little about what it was like to be an intellectual in Romania during the past twenty years. At her research institute, she was one of four people who were not members of the Communist Party. Around 1970 she had been solicited to become a Party member despite her less than perfectly "clean" background (her father had a working-class pedigree, but her mother was bourgeois and had even spent time in jail in the 1950s), because Nicolae Ceauşescu wanted more intellectuals to join. She didn't join, and though it meant she was left out of certain things (she didn't get a fellowship she had applied for, for example), she never regretted it. In some professions, though, especially the press and the other media, people who didn't join the Party were simply thrown out of their jobs. I asked her, "If you had been given that kind of ultimatum, join or leave, would you have joined?"

"Oh, yes, very probably," she answered.

"Were people with bourgeois backgrounds allowed to join?"

"In the early 1970s, yes. But afterward, when there were enough intellectuals in the Party according to Ceauşescu, no."

"What about bourgeois intellectuals who had a sincere allegiance to Marxism?"

"Sincere? There could be no question of that after 1965. It was all a sham," she replied. It reminded me of something Milosz had written: that no Western intellectual, or anyone who hadn't lived through it, could understand what Marxism was like in practice. I mentioned that to Sanda.

"Yes, it's true. Marxism is a beautiful idea," she said, "but it failed."

FRIDAY, MARCH 5

Stalin died forty years ago today. There's a good article in the current issue of *Budapest Week* (an English-language weekly) on the changes that occurred, in Hungary and elsewhere, soon after he died. Imre Nagy, who would later lead the 1956 revolt, became prime minister in 1953, succeeding Rákosi. But Rákosi still maintained power as head of the Communist Party, and in any case the "thaw" didn't last long. By 1954 things were back to what they had been before. Rákosi was in power until the 1956 uprising, at which time he escaped to Moscow and stayed there until his death. In the meantime, László Rajk, who had been hanged as a traitor, was rehabilitated in 1956 and received a new burial. (Rajk's son, an artist and former dissident also named László, is currently a member of Parliament, in the Free Democrat Party.)

Imre Nagy had a similarly roller-coaster career. As the leader of the 1956 uprising, he was hanged in the crackdown that followed, even though he had been a loyal Communist for many years. After his death he became a symbol for all who opposed the regime, and he was formally recognized as a hero two years ago, when his remains received a state funeral. But some people now claim he was in the pay of the Soviet secret police during the 1930s and "sold" many of his friends. This claim hasn't been proved, however. In any case Nagy is no longer the great unifying symbol he once was, because the formerly united opposition groups have broken up into rival parties.

We talked about all this at dinner last night, Robert and I

and Robert's friend Sanyi and Sanyi's "life partner" Margit. (*Élettárs,* such a nice word—it can mean anything from genuine long-term companion to recently acquired live-in girlfriend.) Sanyi is actually Sándor Something or Other, an important official in the Ministry of Justice; Margit is a lawyer. The overall theme of our conversation was "Hungary before and after the Change"—a very delicate matter, since you can't always be sure whether you're speaking to a onetime Party member or a dissident or something in between. Today, of course, everybody would like to have been a dissident, just as in France after the war everybody was suddenly a former member of the Resistance. My sense is that Sanyi and Margit were "in between," like most people. "No one believed in the doctrine anymore, and hadn't for a long time," they said. But between that and open opposition there's a sizable difference.

SATURDAY, MARCH 6

For the first time since I arrived here, this morning I pulled out the folder marked "A Return to Budapest." The first thing that caught my eye was a letter from Mother, dated July 23, 1984; she sent it to me in Paris, giving some addresses and advice about our upcoming trip. Next to it in the folder was the old document I found in the safe in Miami Beach after she died, an official copy of her and Daddy's marriage certificate. I had read this document before and found it very moving, with its spidery handwriting and its "authentic aged" look. It has been folded and unfolded many times, and there's even a small hole in the middle. A big faded brown blotch covers the numbers "910" in Mother's birth date, showing that the numbers have been tampered with. That's the place where someone (She? Daddy? It looks too obvious to have been done by a professional) substituted the 1910 birth date for the authentic 1908 date. I had noted this awkward job of forgery with fond amusement—here was the clear, incontrovertible proof of Mother's vanity! She didn't want anyone to know she was two years older than her husband.

Looking at the document again this morning, I found much more to interest me. The date of this copy is November 19, 1947—they must have gotten it as part of their preparation for leaving Hungary, when they were requesting the exit visa that never came. Did the false birth date get put on while we were still here, so that Mother's passport would carry that instead of 1908? Or did she get the idea later, when we were applying for various papers abroad? I'll never know, but I should get a new copy of the marriage certificate.

The Hungarian term for copies of such documents is very poetic to my American ear: *anyakönyvi kivonat,* "excerpt from the motherbook." Is this diary my "motherbook"? Yes, in more ways than one.

The date of the marriage: July 21, 1936. Mother was just six days shy of her twenty-eighth birthday, which would qualify her as an old maid by the period's standards. Daddy, on the other hand, was a young man—he had just turned twenty-six a month before. What a romantic story, the story of their secret marriage! And yet what I remember most vividly are the fights—so much strife, so little harmony between them during my whole childhood.

There are separate columns on the certificate for information concerning the bride and the groom. The abbreviation *Izr.,* for *Izraelita,* Jewish, appears in both columns. Her address is listed as Akácfa utca 59, in the seventh district, his as Szinyei Something Street 1, in the sixth district. This latter piece of information was completely new to me; I had never noticed it before. I looked under the *ss* in the street list of my Falk map, tenth edition—there, in clear letters, was Szinyei Merse utca, a side street off the upper end of Andrássy Avenue. Number 1 had to be on the corner.

All previous plans for the afternoon were scrapped, and I ended up walking the length of Andrássy Avenue from where I got off the bus. I passed in front of number 60, a beautiful light green building, recently renovated—one would hardly know that for decades it was one of the most dreaded places in Budapest, the headquarters of the secret police, and before that (from 1939 to 1945) the headquarters of the Hungarian Nazi Party, the Arrow Cross (Nyilas). Two plaques placed on the facade in 1991 inform passersby of the building's history, which "may be forgiven but must not be forgotten."

At number 88–90 the avenue broadens out into a circular piazza, with space for four grassy plots and statues of great men. At the four "corners" of the circle are large and very ornate buildings that wrap around from the avenue into side streets. Szinyei Merse is one of those streets. The courtyard at number 1 is a bit smaller and more irregular than the one on the avenue, which has a nice square staircase as you come in, but by now both look badly in need of renovation, as does the whole once-splendid round of buildings on the piazza.

While I was examining the courtyard at number 1, I could see a woman in the shadow near the staircase, evidently the concierge, looking at me. After a few seconds she asked, "Can I help you with something?"

"I'm afraid not. I used to know some people who lived here long ago," I answered. I went over to where she was standing, in the doorway of her apartment.

"Well, I've lived here for forty years, so go ahead and ask me. What's their name?"

"Rubin. When my father got married, this was the address he gave—in 1936."

Her face fell. "That was before my time."

"Have most people in the building lived here very long?"
I asked.

"Yes, everybody."

"Well, thanks anyway." I noticed three large plastic garbage cans near the door on the way out, marked in big white letters: Szinyei Merse 1.

At night after his parents and sisters were in bed, he tiptoed out of the apartment and down the stairs, then stepped onto the dark avenue and turned right toward the Oktogon. The Lukács Café was black and silent like all the other buildings at this late hour. He liked these nightly walks alone, even in cold weather like this. A few hours later he would make the same trip in the other direction, watching the sun rise as he sneaked back home. He and Lili had been married for six months, and nobody knew except her mother—they had had to tell her, or she wouldn't have let him come each night. She kept asking when he would tell his parents, but the time was not right yet. The old man would take it hard. Just that morning he had cornered him before he left for work: "You're a cohen on both sides," he told him for the thousandth time. "Marry that nice girl, and within a year you'll be her father's chief assistant. After he goes, you'll become the rebbe. Do our family proud."

The old man had a fearsome temper. If he found out about the marriage, watch out! Penniless orphan, painted her nails, not a single cohen in the family. Miklós turned up his collar and dug his hands into his coat pockets. Soon he would be warm in Lili's bed. Beautiful blue-eyed Lil, his laughing wife, her hair like a flock of goats in Gilead, her lips like a scarlet thread. The Song of Songs finally made sense, but the yeshiva had not prepared him for this pleasure—the sweetness of it, every night. He felt his flesh rise as he thought about her, his blood rushing as he quickened his steps. The pale-faced rabbi's daughter would have to find herself another groom.

Reading again the letter Mother sent in 1984 made tears come to my eyes. Not for the conventional reasons one could think of, that these are words from beyond the tomb, but because of what she wrote in the beginning: "I was so happy talk to you and received your letter. I can remember Budapest only Svábhegy Normafa vendéglö," and after the word *vendéglö,* restaurant, the letter continues in Hungarian to the end, close to two pages. The passage that made me teary includes the continuation, which I translate: "where every Sunday we ate lunch and we walked there from the cog railway. The Fishermen's Bastion in the Castle in Buda is very beautiful, and Margit Island and the museum at the end of Andrássy Avenue. That is what I remember."

Of course she remembered more; in the next sentence, she mentions that our hiding place in Buda during the war was on Sas Mountain ("but don't go there because it must have a different name by now"—in fact it's the same name, only it's a pretty big neighborhood; I would need a street address), and on the next page she wrote down our address on Acacia Street and the address of the Orthodox Community Bureau where Daddy worked: "But after thirty-five years I don't think there would be anyone there from the old group." So she remembers more, but not much more. At least, and that's what I find so sad, she's not able to gather in writing (would it have been different orally?) more than a few stray items under the heading of what she remembers about Budapest. These few poor fragments, "that is what I remember."

Does it have something to do with the loss of language? Her very first sentence shows that she didn't master English, despite her more than thirty years in the United States. And the moment even these few memories are allowed to appear, she switches to her native tongue: "I hope

you understand my letter, since I wrote it in Hungarian."
Thinking about this, I feel sad and guilty at not having
asked her to talk to me more, not having taped her as I
taped Daddy's sisters, my aunts Rózsi and Hera, last May.
By the time I got around to thinking about taping her, she
was dead, as was her sister, my beloved aunt Magdi; and I
even missed out on Lester, the last of the four siblings.
Thus that whole generation of her family is gone with
hardly a trace. That is what makes me feel like crying, and
what is making me write this diary and undertake pil-
grimages like today's. It's an attempt to recapture something of the dead, for their own sake, but also for mine—to
transmit something of them, and of me (for they are part of
me) to my children. Past and future.

SUNDAY, MARCH 7

Spring is being stubborn about coming, or maybe it's that
winter doesn't want to leave. The temperature has been
around freezing every day this past week; not a sign of any
leaves on the trees. Still, the flower stands are full of tulips
and daffodils and small pots of colorful posies.
    Discovered a new journal yesterday, a liberal monthly
called *Kritika*. The March issue has several articles about
the extreme right and a nice personal essay by György
Konrád, about his experiences last March 15. Evidently
political gatherings and demonstrations occur every year
on that date, since it's a national holiday and the anniversary of the 1848 revolution. Last year Konrád gave a speech
for the Free Democrats in one place and was applauded;
then he and his friend the film director Károly Makk went
to a different gathering, and there he was surrounded by
faces full of hate. People jeered at him, made jokes: "Long
live György Konrád, the greatest Hungarian writer—but
not for long." (The nasty play on words comes across bet-

ter in Hungarian.) After a while the two men had to hurry to their car, where they were surrounded by a band of skinheads; they barely got away without a fight. Konrád writes: "No one looked at me like that during the Communist period. Even the political police showed some respect; they read our works in their office, we had some effect on them. They were almost embarrassed, sometimes, to do their job with us." He wonders, ironically, how he went from being the "Number One Enemy of the Kádár regime to being the Number One Enemy of the Antall regime." (Joseph Antall is the prime minister, leader of the MDF.)

MONDAY, MARCH 8

Ungvár, my grandparents' birthplace, is not listed on a Hungarian map. That's because its name is now Uzhgorod, and it's in Ukraine. Dora, the Collegium's librarian, helped me look it up on the map today, and she told me a well-known joke about Ungvár: A man says he was born in Hungary, grew up in Poland, went to school in Slovakia, and got his first job in Ukraine. His listener replies, "Well, you've certainly moved around a lot!" "Not at all," he says, "I've never left Ungvár." A story of postmodern identities *avant la lettre* if I ever heard one. This whole region is full of shifting borders, with no necessary connection between language, ethnic identification, and nationality. Imagine being born in Munkács but coming of age in Mukačevo, or being born in Kolozsvár but growing up in Cluj. Proper names, one would think, are the most stable, the least subject to change. Yet here are the names of cities totally transformed, and often transformed again, depending on the geopolitics of the moment. It's unsettling, worse than moving to a new apartment. More like shedding your skin or acquiring false papers.

The Center of Europe

Went to the Ecseri Piac, Budapest's flea market, with Julie and her cousin this morning. The market spreads out over a huge space, and as usual there's everything from pure junk to expensive porcelain and furniture. I bought three coffee mugs made of Zsolnay porcelain, from the city of Pécs. They're decorated with hand-painted scenes of the Three Graces—I bought them because they reminded me of cups we had when I was a child. "Ah, the power of nostalgia," Julie said, but she had bought some nostalgic pottery of her own.

Julie's cousin told us Andrássy Avenue has changed its name four times in the past fifty years! Right after the war it became Stalin Avenue, then after 1956 Hungarian Youth Avenue, then People's Republic Avenue, and finally, after 1989, Andrássy Avenue again. "It's a perfect symbol of what has happened to this country since the war. Back to zero," he said with a bitter smile. He's about my age, was trained as a social worker, but now owns a lucrative business. He strikes me as the model of Milosz's Central European intellectual: sardonic, ironically aware of his and his country's "inferior" status in relation to the West, anti-Marxist because he has seen what it was like to live under Marxism—and altogether charming.

Later I met Werner, our German fellow at the Collegium, who's an art historian and a specialist in architecture; he showed me the almost restored synagogue on Rumbach Street, a very large and impressive brick structure built around 1890. It's in the eclectic style, with an Oriental accent: twin towers that look like minarets. I hadn't known about this synagogue, thinking there were only two in the neighborhood: the big, showy Reform one on Dohány Street, which is now in the last stages of restoration, and "ours," the Orthodox one on Kazinczy Street, somewhat more modest but still impressive and quite large. This third one is splendid, built during the golden age of Jewish prosperity before the turn of the century. That this tiny neighborhood could support three major synagogues shows how proud and weighty the Jewish community in Budapest was during those years.

And now? The Rumbach Street synagogue, once restored, will be converted to another use.

THURSDAY, MARCH 11

Tibor's wife, Anna, lent me a book on the history of Hungarian Jewry from 1526 to 1949, by László Gonda. In the back there's a detailed chronology, from which I got the following statistics: In 1869, when the great flowering of Austro-Hungarian culture and commerce began, 542,279 Jews lived in Hungary; 30 percent were "city dwellers," meaning Budapest and other cities. By 1910 the number of Jews had grown to 911,227; more than 50 percent of them were city dwellers, and 77 percent claimed Hungarian as their mother tongue. (The other 23 percent didn't necessarily speak Yiddish, like the Jews of Poland—they could have been Romanian or Czech speakers, since Hungary included large parts of what are now those countries.) The Trianon Peace Treaty after World War I chopped off more than half of Hungary's territory, also shrinking the Jewish population. The 1920 census showed only 473,355 Jews, 73 percent of them urban and more than 95 percent claiming Hungarian as their mother tongue. In 1949, the last year the census asked about religion, the number had shrunk a great deal more, thanks to Hitler and his Arrow Cross sympathizers: 133,862, just about all of them living in Budapest and speaking Hungarian as their mother tongue. Those in the provinces had been almost totally wiped out.

The first political anti-Semitic movement in Hungary

began in 1875, when a certain Gyözö Istóczy, "an until then virtually unknown representative of the ruling party in Parliament, demanded that the Minister of the Interior say what he intended to do about the flood of foreign Jewish immigrants settling in the country, and whether he would object to the founding of a self-protection movement by non-Jews" (p. 321). In 1878 this same Istóczy suggested that all the Hungarian Jews should be resettled in Palestine. In 1882 a famous blood trial (in Nyíregyháza, Mother's birthplace!) involving the drowning death of a young girl brought about numerous anti-Semitic riots, both before and after the "not guilty" verdict. In 1883 the Anti-Semitic Party was founded, its program consisting in "breaking the power of the Jews and resisting Jewish influence." And so on and so on, in an all too familiar and depressing pattern. Things got worse during World War I, and much worse right after the Béla Kun regime. In 1920 the *numerus clausus* was instituted, limiting the number of Jews who could be admitted to the university. Jew beatings in the university were not uncommon.

That reminds me of another puzzle I found in my "Return to Budapest" folder: the piece of paper on which Milton, Mother's distant cousin, scribbled what he knew about her family last May, as we sat at the kitchen table at my sister Judy's house the day after my niece's bat mitzvah. I had told Milton I would be coming to Budapest and would try to track down some of the family past, so he took a piece of lined paper we found in a drawer and drew a rough family tree of the Lebowitzes, Mother's maternal family, accompanied by a few parenthetical notations. A single sentence jumped out at me when I saw it again a few days ago: next to the name of my grandfather Moshe Stern (who married my grandmother Raizl Lebowitz) is the remark "Died c. 1919, result of beating by Hungary Firster."

I had always been told, by Mother and Grandmother

and everyone else I can remember, that my grandfather died of a stroke. My image of him, the solemn, rotund mustached man whose enlarged portrait hung in Grandmother's room next to a matching one of her as a young matron about 1910, was that of a man who had died young, the way some men keel over with a heart attack before they're forty. Suddenly that story is replaced by one of anti-Semitic violence. Did he find himself, by bad luck, in the way of fascist thugs? Was he perhaps involved in a street demonstration? The year 1919 was the date of the Béla Kun government: Did he have something to do with that?

Which version of his death is the myth, which the reality? If Milton's story is true, it would add a whole new dimension to my passionate interest in the history of nationalism and anti-Semitism in Hungary.

FRIDAY, MARCH 12

Yesterday afternoon I met Frances, an American Fulbright scholar who's here for a year teaching American literature at the university. We had met briefly in the States a couple of times, so she called when she heard I was in Budapest. She's an interesting woman, very independent, not afraid to try new things from what I can see. She's totally fascinated by Hungarian cinema, even trying to learn Hungarian so that she can understand films without subtitles. We went to see Péter Gothár's first film, *Ajándék ez a nap*, *This Day Is a Gift*, made in 1979. I had never heard of Gothár until I saw *Time Stands Still*, probably his best-known film. Frances told me about this one, and I'm awfully glad—it's wonderful. Basically it's about an apartment. The young heroine is having an affair with a married man, and their dream is to find a "place to share." In the end she loses interest in the man but still has the apartment. The film dates from just about the time things were getting looser in the economy, and one has the impression of a great many deals, shady and otherwise, being made in real estate and elsewhere.

The best part, really extraordinary, is the last long sequence, where the heroine and her ex-lover's wife spend a night drinking and confiding in each other. The wife, a mousy young woman with a childish voice, was played by an actress who seemed to live the role. At the end, lying next to her friend on the bed munching chips, she says: "It feels like a train, with Atti [her husband] and the children waving on the platform. I like this train." When the heroine asks her, "Can you hear me?" she answers, "No, I can only hear myself eating. It's really something, from the inside, come and listen"—and she leans over, trying to get the other woman to hear her inner sound.

It's hard to capture in words, but the effect of this scene was both hilarious and uplifting. Here are two women struggling to cope with their daily lives, sharing a privileged moment of intimacy (not eroticism; the film avoids that possibility), all the more extraordinary because they've been "rivals." Both women are aware that their friendship is more important than their relationship with the husband. I was especially impressed because the only other film I've seen by Gothár didn't suggest a feminist sensibility. Neither have any of the other Hungarian films (admittedly, not many) I've seen so far, with the possible exception of Márta Mészáros's work. But I would call this scene feminist in the best sense: focusing on women from the inside, not hostile to men, but for once willing to put them out of the picture (literally).

In the evening I went to a party given by another American Fulbright professor, in a big old apartment in Pest. Lots of people there, including many Hungarians. I met a woman who teaches philosophy at the university, Ilona, and her husband, Gábor, a documentary filmmaker who's making a film on Budapest architecture. He's very knowledgeable, and we spoke for a long time. "It would be impossible to accomplish today the technical feats builders accomplished in Budapest between 1867 and 1912," Gábor said. "There simply aren't enough trained craftsmen who could do that kind of work in so short a time. Just think, the Music Academy was built and completely decorated, outside and inside, mosaics and all, in something like ten years." The Music Academy is justly famous for its interior decorations, done about 1890. I asked whether there's a general plan to renovate the inner city. He shrugged: "Not really. Now that most of the apartment buildings are no longer state owned, the city's hoping the owners will have the work done. But obviously that won't happen in most cases, since it's so expensive." Gábor is a very attractive man, tall and athletic looking, with sparkling eyes and a beautiful smile. Why do I always notice these things? Stupid question—Who doesn't? But it's also part of Mother's legacy. The first thing she always noticed about people was their looks and how they were dressed.

SATURDAY, MARCH 13

Red-white-and-green Hungarian flags have appeared on storefronts and buildings all over the city, in preparation for the March 15 holiday. All the bookstores are displaying Petőfi's picture next to his "National Song" (the great patriotic poem, recited every year at official celebrations) and the list of demands formulated by the revolutionaries in March 1848: freedom of the press, a separate Parliament, self-determination. The revolution was put down brutally by the Austrians and their Russian allies, but it's celebrated as a national holiday nonetheless. Monday morning there will be a big parade to the National Museum, where the revolution started. But I won't be there, because the Collegium is going en masse to Esztergom and Visegrád that day. "A class outing, how darling!" Eva exclaimed when I told her about it on the phone last night. It really is a class outing—we're even having our teacher along, for Werner will give us a learned tour of the Esztergom cathedral, and we have also obtained special permission to visit the excavations of King Mátyás's castle in Visegrád, where one of the excavation leaders will explain what they've been doing. This excursion came about as a result of our fellows' meeting two weeks ago, so everyone feels very positive and proprietary about it.

The only other news at the moment is that the poet Vörösmarty's monument in the middle of his square has been unwrapped from its burlap covering—a sure sign of spring. The monument is a large stone creation showing the poet seated, gazing benignly at the *küzdö nép*, the bravely struggling Hungarian people—old men, mothers and children, old women—who form a human chain on both sides of him. The only writing on the monument is a quotation from one of Vörösmarty's poems, about what the homeland expects from a true Magyar. No doubt about it, patriotism is a very strong sentiment in this country.

LATER

I've just returned from an evening organized by MAZSIKE, an acronym for Hungarian Jewish Cultural Association. Tibor was among the speakers—it was a program about Hungarian Jews and the 1848 revolution. The first half was the artistic part, with music, recitation of poetry and other texts, including an archpatriotic sermon preached by a famous rabbi in July 1848, addressing the first Jewish battalion of the revolution, and a very fine polemic by Petöfi, written after the anti-Semitic outbursts of April 1848, up-braiding the rabble-rousers.

The second half of the program consisted of a round-table with three historians, among them Tibor. A roly-poly man dressed in denim overalls gave a wonderful short speech, asking whether the great patriotism of the Jews in 1848 had been naive. It could appear so from today's per-spective, he said—but at the time the Jews' push toward as-similation was quite logical. The Hungary they wanted to consider their *haza*, their homeland, was the Hungary of 1848, whose motto was "Freedom and Dignity for All." The tragedy, he said, is that Jews did not always realize that those two concepts, Hungarianness and freedom, were not necessarily one. That's what Jews today must be watchful about, he concluded: only as long as Hungarianness and freedom are not divorced from each other should Jews pledge their allegiance to Hungary. I really liked the way he delivered his speech, clear and strong; and I like the argu-ment too.

Tibor, who went last, had only one big point to make: compared with neighboring countries that also had na-tionalist movements at the time, Hungarian nationalists were the least anti-Semitic. Indeed, in his opinion the best of the Hungarian intelligentsia were always philo-Semitic, right up to the Shoah. They disapproved of the anti-Jewish laws, both before the war and during.

At that point an angry voice cried out from the back: "Not all the intellectuals!"

"Oh, yes," Tibor insisted.

"Right—all except those that didn't," came the mocking reply. Unfortunately there was no opportunity to discuss this question with the audience; the heckler from the back was silenced, and the program ended after one more musi-cal number by a virtuoso violinist. It reminded me of the "Evening with Miklós Vajda," where audience participation was also quashed, though probably not for the same reason (tonight it was to avoid a bitter debate).

I wonder why Tibor wants so badly to deny the obvious, that there have always been anti-Semites among intellectuals, in Hungary as elsewhere. Louis-Ferdinand Céline, one of France's truly innovative and original writers, was a rabid anti-Semite. It's terrible, but there's no point in pretending it's not true. Tibor might claim that no *true* intellectual can be anti-Semitic, since anti-Semitism is such a low, ignoble passion. Maybe he is thinking of himself, a non-Jewish intellectual who abhors anti-Semitism. I wish he were right.

SUNDAY, MARCH 14

Walk up János Mountain with Tibor and Anna, and back down again. We walked on a paved road most of the way, talking. Tibor has been working on the historical sociology of Hungarian Jews and is a well of information. I told them about my grandfather Stern; Tibor said I should be able to find his death certificate in the archives of the Orthodox Community Bureau. It's quite possible he was beaten to death, because between July 1919 and March 1920 there was open season on Jews, following the downfall of the Kun government. It was especially bad in the provinces, where the "Whites" (soldiers in uniform, who didn't represent the government but were tolerated by it) would often show up in a village, ask where the Jews lived, drag the men out, and shoot or hang them or beat them to death. But my grandfather is buried in Budapest, I told Tibor. The beatings were less frequent in Budapest, but they happened there too, he said.

Around 4:00 P.M., I went to meet Julie at the Pilvax Café, where a large group of writers, journalists, and assorted intellectuals were holding a meeting to defend the freedom of the press. They had chosen the Pilvax because the 1848 revolution had started there—Petőfi wrote his "National Song" there, and it was from there the revolutionaries started their march to the National Museum. I arrived just as the meeting was breaking up, but Julie filled me in. The background to this meeting is the current feud, which has been going on for several months, over who controls the national radio and television stations. The two appointed directors were relieved of their posts last November by Prime Minister Joseph Antall, who didn't find them sufficiently pro-government. But President Árpád Göncz supports them and claims his constitutional right as the only one who can fire them. There's a lot at stake because of the coming election campaign, in which radio and TV will play a major role.

The group that had called the meeting was the Democratic Charta, a nonpartisan umbrella organization that sees itself as a defender of civil rights and democratic values. Before I came they had been talking about drawing up a "twelve points" document, just like the one of 1848, demanding freedom of the press along with other rights. But in the end they decided to drop the idea because nobody had a good enough document to propose. Just stick to the old one, somebody said.

I saw the novelist György Konrád toward the front of the room—he looked just like his photo in last week's *Kritika*. Closer by, I recognized one of the speakers from last night, the one who spoke about Hungarianness and freedom. I told him how much I had liked his remarks, which seemed to come "straight from the heart." He looked very pleased.

On the way to the Petőfi monument, where the next part of the meeting was to take place, Julie and I found ourselves walking next to a large man who struck up a conversation and appointed himself our guide. His name is András; he teaches law in college, is polite to the point of gallantry (he stopped at a flower vendor to buy both of us small bunches of lily of the valley), and seems to know everything there is to know about Budapest. He told us more about the Democratic Charta: it was founded in August 1992 in response to the "Csurka scandal," which is how people refer to the nationalist/anti-Semitic pamphlet István Csurka published at that time. More than 100,000 people showed up at the rally called by the Charta a few days later—that rally was also held at the Petöfi statue.

There was a large crowd today, although not 100,000. The featured speaker, Elemir Hankiss (he's the ousted TV director and a well-known sociologist) gave a very good speech, with some literary flourishes one would never find at a political rally in America. "What would Petöfi say if his frozen statue suddenly came to life and he found himself among us today?" Hankiss began. He then sprinkled his speech with lines from Petöfi's poetry, which he obviously expected his listeners to recognize. The political content of the speech was that Hungarians are now realizing that freedom, the noble watchword of opponents of the Communist regime, does not automatically bring with it peace and prosperity for all. Much work and struggle lie ahead before those ideals are realized; freedom implies not only rights but responsibilities.

At the end of his speech everyone sang the Hungarian national anthem, and I realized I knew neither the words nor the melody. Julie stood beside me, singing along. How come she knew it and I didn't? One more sign of how completely we cut the ties with Hungary when we left. In some ways it's a source of strength, to be able to shrug off the past repeatedly, as if each new place were a new life: the less baggage, the more easily you make your way. But it's also an impoverishment to leave so much behind. My return to Budapest may be nothing else than an attempt to find once again some of the treasures—even the poor ones, maybe especially the poor ones—we let drop.

WEDNESDAY, MARCH 17

The Collegium had its "class outing" on Monday, a great success despite the continuing cold weather. We tramped around the ruins of King Mátyás's summer palace in Visegrád, which had nothing summery about it that day. The palace's exact whereabouts were not known until sixty years ago, and its very existence was considered in doubt by some historians because it had been completely buried by sliding earth. Yet it was a truly magnificent complex of buildings in the late fifteenth century, designed and decorated by the greatest Italian and Italian-trained architects, painters, sculptors, and stonecutters. Its gardens extended all the way down to the Danube, so that visitors could arrive by boat and walk directly up to be greeted by the king. We learned all this from an art historian involved in the excavation work, a young woman who explained many details. The first excavations began in 1935, and a great deal of further work has gone on over the past ten years.

When she told us the story of how the palace fell into ruin after Mátyás's reign and then was buried by the mountain, Tibor gave a bitter laugh. "Typical of Hungary," he said. It's true, a fifteenth-century palace of that grandeur would very likely not have suffered the same fate in France or Italy. As someone pointed out, that's the kind of thing one expects to hear about places two thousand years old, not five hundred. Hungary fell enormously after Mátyás, and the 150 years of Turkish rule in the sixteenth and seventeenth centuries didn't help.

In Esztergom, Werner gave us a guided tour of the museum next to the hulking basilica built in the nineteenth century. I found the basilica ugly—too big, graceless—but the site is wonderful. It overlooks the Danube, only a stone's throw from Slovakia on the other side. The remains of a bridge bombed during the war and never rebuilt are still visible. That too may be a symbol, I suppose.

Today we had our second Collegium seminar, with Robert leading a discussion of his new book. Farkas and the rector were there, very Prospero and Ariel, and they both came to dinner afterward. Exceptionally, we had a small number at dinner and spoke mostly Hungarian. Farkas is an extraordinary man, not only a great scholar but a true mensch, very widely read and with a good sense of humor. He told me he was a teenager during the war and lost his father to the Nazis. I would have liked to ask him more, but realized it's a subject he doesn't want to talk about at length. The rector's family is not Jewish, but they too suffered during the war. They were from Transylvania and had to leave their home—they settled farther north and never went back. As far as I can tell, the rector has two passions, tennis and music. He plays tennis every day, quite a feat given his schedule; and he goes to concerts two or three times a week. He's a delightful man, and his good humor is positively infectious.

As for Tibor—multilingual, cynical, dogmatic Tibor—I like him a lot because he's so smart. I said to him tonight, as we were leaving the restaurant and he made some particularly sardonic remark: "You're the most cynical man I've ever met."

"Yes, I know. My mother always tells me that," he replied with a straight face.

SATURDAY, MARCH 20

Julie left today, back to her work and family in Toronto. I'm really going to miss her; we've become good friends in a surprisingly short time. We talked about that over lunch yesterday, how rare it is at our age. The Hungarian connection and the Jewish connection together make for a very strong bond. But aside from that, there's the personal chemistry. Mysterious, how that works: with some people an immediate connection; with others, indifference or even repulsion. (The French speak about *atomes crochues*, "hooked atoms," a perfectly apt image.)

Last Tuesday I went with Julie to the opening of Yoko Ono's art exhibition at the National Gallery. It was quite the fashionable place to be, with hundreds of people milling about, drinking white wine or club soda—the scene could have been in London, New York, Paris. We saw the painter László Fehér, whom we both know a little, standing impassively next to his wife as the crowd swirled around them. He took us to see the painting of his that's hanging in the gallery, acquired a few years ago. It's a large painting in the dark neoexpressionist mode, quite different from his current work (which I prefer, actually: large, flat planes and outlines of figures that look like memory traces—very evocative). "I'm next to Baselitz," Fehér said proudly, pointing to the painting next to his. "I'm also in Aachen, where I'm next to . . ." and so on, in a way I found not obnoxious but rather endearing. Instead of saying "I have a painting here or in Aachen, and it's next to a work by X," he said "I am next to X," as if both he and X were their paintings and could multiply themselves and be present wherever their works are. A lovely image.

Yoko Ono, looking stylish in black tights and a black jacket, her hair cut short, arrived late and was immediately surrounded by journalists and microphones. I didn't even try to get near, but Julie managed to talk to her because she's reviewing the opening for her paper. The show is called "Endangered Species," referring to people. The most powerful piece was a large sculpture in a black matte material, showing four life-size figures sitting on a bench, naked, their heads hanging down and necks cut at the nape. A man, a woman, a little girl, and a young boy, they all have labels tied to their wrists or ankles as if they were exhibits in a museum. They could be figures caught in some nuclear conflagration, preserved in charred form. Fehér said: "That's good. I wish I had done that."

SUNDAY, MARCH 21

First day of spring, and I'm home with a cold. Outside it's a brilliant day of sunshine; the temperature is due to rise into the sixties.

Overheard at the Gellért baths yesterday morning: One young American woman to her four friends, all of them huddling comfortably in the warm water: "Hungarian has the same word for pickle and cucumber—*uborka*." I don't know why that made a strong impression on me, but it did. Maybe because of the contrast between the familiar way the five Americans (they looked like "nice college girls") had taken to the naked Central European baths and the estrangement they feel from the language. Still, that young woman was learning Hungarian—she pronounced *uborka* well, not as if she had just read it on a menu. It's fascinating to me, breaking all my old myths, that one can actually learn Hungarian (and want to learn it) without being born into it.

Lunch conversation on Thursday, with Eva and two of her colleagues from the university: the question of taxis came up, and the Hungarians all said they rarely took one—too expensive. "What about theater and concert tickets; are they expensive too?" I asked. "Absolutely," replied a lively woman who has about four different jobs teaching French. "If you count three tickets at 300 forints, that's almost 1,000.

And with the salary of an academic . . ." Before 1989 a
ticket for the balcony of the Music Academy cost 10 forints. Now it costs 250. Same thing with books; they're becoming too expensive for most people. I suddenly felt
guilty, like an "ugly American," for thinking that everything in Budapest is so cheap and taking taxis whenever I
feel like it.

I asked whether they thought anyone regretted the old
regime. Yes, they said, some people do—those on pen-
sions, those who have lost their jobs, those whose standard
of living is sinking every day. "At the Institute, our budget
not only hasn't increased, it was drastically cut this year,"
Eva said. Yet I'm sure she doesn't regret the ancien régime,
for she always speaks of it with heavy irony. Before we
went to lunch, she took me into her office with one of her
colleagues and pulled out three framed portraits of Lenin
from various cupboards and drawers. "Just think, all three
used to be on the wall!" she chuckled.

LATER

My cold was better this evening, so I went out and met Julie's and my "Budapest guide" András at the theater. We
saw Árpád Göncz's *Kö a kövön, Stone on Stone*—truly interesting, and not only because its author is the current president of Hungary. It's a two-character play, about a man and
a woman who were once lovers and who meet again in Budapest more than twenty years after she left the country (in
1956). An evening of confrontation about their lives, their
relation to Hungary, to history. The woman is Jewish; her
father was a lawyer killed by the Arrow Cross in the last
year of the war. She now lives in San Francisco, married to
a psychiatrist. Her husband's a wonderful man but has no
idea what it means to be an Eastern European. "When I
told him about the Rajk trial, he said Rajk should have got-

ten himself a good lawyer who could have saved him!" she says mockingly. Everybody in the audience laughed like crazy.

The male character is of Hungarian peasant stock, a biologist. He was involved in the 1956 uprising and spent a few years in jail; now he's married to a woman he doesn't love but who has shared his destiny. Destiny and history are recurrent themes between these two characters. She reproaches him for not having left with her in 1956. He speaks about belonging to this land. She speaks about her father and grandfather, who thought there would be room for them in this land but were wrong. There's a powerful sense in the play that both of these people enounce "good" values, and also a sense of tragedy that they parted, since they were passionately in love.

It's a very honest and thought-provoking work, which premiered in 1991. András said it couldn't have been performed before "the Change" because of the harsh way it talks about 1956 and what followed.

András reminds me, curiously, of my uncle Lester: same rotund shape and round face with glasses, same jovial manner. He is slightly slovenly in appearance the way some fat men are, even though he wears a suit and tie. Although only in his mid-forties, he looks much older. He's extremely cultivated, knows European literature and music in depth, and seems to know the history of practically every stone in Budapest. He loves to tell witty anecdotes, many of them by or about Budapest writers. He admits he's extremely neurotic, of course. He fits perfectly what I'm beginning to think of as the standard image of the Central European intellectual: humorous, pessimistic, cultured, lacking in self-confidence, and at the same time very opinionated. But really I should say the Central European Jewish intellectual, for this particular mixture of intelligence, cultivation, and self-irony strikes me as very Jewish.

He's worried about what's happening in Eastern Europe. "We're between Sarajevo and Dantzig, sitting ducks for any number of explosions. Your parents were right to leave when they did," he said. He himself would never leave, though: "I wouldn't last one minute in America— the stress would kill me!" He was married, briefly, to a woman he didn't love and who didn't love him. Has a daughter, now fifteen, to whom he's devoted. "The truth is, I've never really been in love," he said. "I'm too selfish in love, though not in friendship."

TUESDAY, MARCH 23

The Hungarian-American seder Robert and I are organizing is taking shape nicely. András will be there, as well as Tibor and Anna. Today I invited the art historian Judit (I had met her in New York) and her family, husband and two children; she was positively delighted. "We don't do it, and we really miss it," she said.

"Did your family do it when you were a child?" I asked.

"No, my father didn't do anything. But I still miss it!" They've been to some seders in the States, but never to one in Budapest. That's what it means to be an assimilated Jew, I guess.

WEDNESDAY, MARCH 24

Second visit with my scholar-editor acquaintance János this morning, almost as long as the first! We spoke Hungarian this time, and talked a lot about the current situation here. My head was spinning by the time I left, he mentioned so many names and details I wanted to retain.

He looked somewhat younger today, and in fact mentioned he was born after the war. His manner was still charming and somewhat scatterbrained, but not quite so "boyishly bumbling" as last time—and certainly not after we went into his study, where the really intense conversation began. "What do you think about the extreme right? Are you worried?" I asked him.

"No, I'm not. I'm optimistic," he answered. That's because, in his opinion, things are very different from the 1930s. Most important, there's now a counteroffensive to nationalism and anti-Semitism. "We're here too," he said.

"Well, there were people who opposed Nazism in the 1930s," I pointed out. He didn't respond to that.

I was wondering whether he would mention his father, and to my great joy he did. "My father was a hard-line Communist, the editor of *Szabad Nép* [*Free People*, the official Party paper] after the war and even before, when it was an underground paper. He was the nemesis of many a writer—chief censor." I wanted to ask him how it felt, personally, to be the son of his father, but I hesitated. Finally, much later, when I was almost ready to go, I did ask him—and the conversation went on for close to another hour! One thing that saves his father in János's eyes is that he supported the 1956 uprising and was against the Russian invasion. He was never tried with the other fifty-sixers, János says, because of his past as an orthodox Party member; but he left the Party after 1956, or was excluded—I no longer remember which. "Lucky for me," János laughed.

Of course this version of his father's career may be somewhat slanted. But it's still very interesting, from a human standpoint.

About anti-Semitism, János was categorical: "It's time to become aggressive. Paradoxically, I've become much more aware of being a Jew because of it—you know Hungarian

Jews have generally been very assimilated, and my family certainly was. But this changes things." His idea is to write an article in which he will defend not the idea of tolerance ("Let's be good Magyars and tolerate difference, those who are not like us"), but rather the idea of a "loose" Hungarianness: "I'm not Magyar the way Petőfi was—and if Csurka's a Magyar, then I'm not one at all. We should love difference, not tolerate it," he said. I liked that.

SUNDAY, MARCH 28—PARIS

Arrived here on Friday morning, for a week—a good time to get some perspective on Budapest.

Taxi ride in Paris, looking at the belle epoque buildings with a new eye. These are really stone, not merely stucco imitation—but the decorations often remind me of Budapest. It felt on many levels as if Paris were "the real thing"—like a long and generally happy marriage one returns to after a passionate fling. Feeling slightly guilty, perhaps, but above all relieved to find the marriage still works; that one is, after all, home. Paradox, that for me it should be the adopted city that functions as home while the native city is the latecoming, interloping passion.

From here, Budapest and all its concerns seem like distant planets. Who in these parts has even heard of István Csurka, much less knows what he represents? Once I explain, people are interested—but I suspect they find it all terribly exotic. Curious, that I've suddenly become an expert on Hungary. I realized, talking about Budapest at a dinner with French friends the other night, that I now know a great deal about Hungarian history, literature, and current politics, which I hadn't the slightest inkling of two months ago. One of the guests at the dinner, a witty and charming man, is a Hungarian who left Budapest in 1956 when he was in his teens and goes back often because his parents still live there (near Margit Bridge). He knows Hungarian well and can still recite some poems by heart, but he knows almost nothing about what's happening in or around Hungary politically right now. He hadn't even heard of George Soros!

Quiet Days on the Danube

Back in Budapest, and it feels like home. I came on the same plane from Paris as Saul Bellow, who gave a lecture at the Collegium this evening. He's traveling with his wife, a friendly woman who must be in her thirties or early forties; he's seventy-eight. Curious, these May-December marriages: the Very Famous Old Man, feted and wined and dined, with his young, solicitous, adoring wife. I can't imagine myself in that role, though it must have its satisfying aspects.

Bellow's lecture, "Intellectuals and the Cold War," was attended by an overflow crowd. He began with some personal reminiscences about his childhood and family, Russian immigrants to Montreal, then Chicago; they left Russia a few years before the revolution. He was a Trotskyite as a young man and actually saw Trotsky minutes after he was killed! He and a friend traveling in Mexico had an appointment to visit him, and he was killed that very day. Bellow and his friend went to the hospital (the police thought they were reporters, Bellow said) and saw him while his corpse was still warm. Astounding that they were allowed to enter his room, total strangers, after an assassination.

The rest of the talk was more analytical, about intellectuals and politics—fairly straightforward anti-Communism, condemning Sartre and other French intellectuals for their willful blindness about the Soviet Union. I understood Bellow's argument to be that writers shouldn't get involved in politics, but later over dinner he said he meant they *needn't* get involved; and they should never toe a party line. Generally, party lines don't make for good literature. I agree with that.

It has become very fashionable, among some American intellectuals, to condemn the misguided Europeans who went along with the Soviets after the war. But it's easy for us, looking back, to see the evils of Stalinism; to those living through that time, in the West at any rate (those in the Soviet Union knew the score by then), things may have looked very different. I should have asked Bellow: "And what about today? How do you feel about feminism, women's studies, multiculturalism?" The Cold War is ancient history now. Where does he place himself with current issues? Not on my side, I would guess.

Although I don't agree with his politics, I continue to admire the creator of Herzog and Augie March. Bellow may be right—writers shouldn't get involved in politics.

THURSDAY, APRIL 8

Very successful seder on Monday—there were seventeen of us around the table in my living room. None of the Hungarians knew how to read Hebrew, and I'm sure several had never set foot in a synagogue or attended a seder. András positively beamed when we sang songs, but he clearly had no idea what was going on. Fascinating! There seems to be no middle ground here for Jewish identity—one is either a practicing Jew with all the trimmings or else totally ignorant. Yet András feels very strongly that he's Jewish. But it's because of anti-Semitism, like János. Ironic, that it should be anti-Semites who goad Jews into feeling Jewish. It means there's no positive content to their Jewishness, only a negative sense of exclusion or (in the worst case) persecution.

It was my turn to lead the fellows' seminar at the Collegium today. I did an introduction to feminist criticism, and as one example I had distributed my essay on Bataille's

Story of the Eye. Good discussion, everyone felt at ease, which allowed for some heated exchanges. Did I ever feel the abyss that separates West (more particularly, the United States) from East in these matters!

Stani was outraged: "This kind of thing makes me move close to fundamentalism!" he fumed. "None of this has anything to do with the problems of survival—it's all luxury stuff!" His religious Catholic side was shocked too: "What's all this about the mother being a sexual being? I have a mother, and I never thought such things about her!" It was quite charming, his indignation was so heartfelt. According to him, psychoanalytic interpreters, even feminists like me, are obsessed by sex: "Why do you say that Baudelaire's line about 'pink and black jewel' refers to the woman's genitals? Why not say the same thing about *The Red and the Black*?" I explained to him about the psychoanalytic interpretations of jewels and the whole tradition of erotic literature that uses jewels as a metaphor for the female sex, but he wasn't buying it. Then Robert launched into a diatribe against people who claim something is valid just because it comes from a particular source, as opposed to objective validation. It wasn't clear what this had to do with the discussion, but it's a pet idea of his.

Afterward we went to dinner at the Tabáni Kakas, where I sat next to Stani and Sanda, with Anna nearby. We women ganged up on Stani, but he was good-natured about it. It was a highly successful evening, even though I suspect some people now think of feminist literary criticism (and maybe of me too) as outlandish and unserious.

Danny arrives tomorrow morning for a ten-day visit.

MONDAY, APRIL 12

Easter Monday, and everything is closed except a few museums. I was going to take Danny, but his cold has gotten worse—he was already sniffling when he got off the plane. We decided he should stay in bed until evening and drink lots of lemon tea. He's reading a long novel by Erich Segal and is not too unhappy to be spending the day in bed.

Yesterday we made our pilgrimage to Acacia Street and climbed the three flights again at number 59. We toyed with the idea of knocking on the door like last time but decided against it. We looked down into the courtyard from the stone balustrade but did not take pictures. It felt easier to be in the building with Danny than by myself. An old lady stared at us through her closed window on the ground floor, but it didn't matter. Afterward we walked over to Andrássy Avenue, to the Müvész Café for some tea and pastries. Danny liked the creamy *krémes* a lot and also ate a poppyseed strudel, *mákos rétes*. Then he ordered the same two again! His appetite has been huge since he arrived in Budapest, bless him. He really went for the roast goose at the Tabáni Kakas the other night.

It's interesting, seeing Budapest through Danny's eyes. Aside from the house on Acacia Street, he remembers nothing about our 1984 visit except perhaps the Gellért's outdoor wave pool, which is not open yet. He's impressed by how little everything costs in American terms, but he also notices, much more than I, just how run-down and poor things look. He finds the Russian-made Ladas we see parked at every curb uniform and tinny, and what he notices most about the turn-of-the-century buildings around Andrássy Avenue is how dirty they are. I suspect he thinks I'm slightly nuts, comparing Budapest to Paris!

SUNDAY, APRIL 18

Danny left today; I took him to the airport at 6:00 A.M.

He never ceases to delight me, and to surprise me too. A few days ago we went to the small Jewish museum in the big synagogue on Dohány Street. Three rooms are devoted to ritual and everyday objects of all kinds, but the really compelling room is the last one, commemorating the Holocaust in Hungary. The persecution started here very late, but once it started it went fast. To complement the Nazis' work, Budapest had its homegrown variety of Jew-haters who went around shooting people for sport. (The Hollywood film of a few years ago, *The Music Box*, evokes that time rather well; on a much larger scale, so does György Konrád's recent autobiographical novel *A Feast in the Garden*.)

Daniel took in all the exhibits in the room without saying much, from the wartime posters with inscriptions like "Shame on you for buying from a Jew!" to the display cases showing dresses and underwear made out of Torah covers and prayer shawls. I was truly shocked by those—as if people who didn't hesitate to make soap out of other human beings would hesitate to make panties out of a prayer shawl. After we got home, Daniel sat down at my computer and wrote several pages describing the visit to the museum and grappling with the question of racism in Eastern Europe, past and present. I was very proud of him. Underneath the fifteen-year-old, at times uncommunicative, exterior a lot of thinking goes on.

And Michael? He's fighting his demons, not coming to Budapest. I talk to him often, running up astronomical phone bills to Los Angeles.

It's strange, but living here so far away from the boys has allowed me to focus almost all my attention on myself, as if I were truly "single," with no dependents. Yet they're always there in the background, and if I don't talk to them for more than three days in a row I begin to feel anxious. I've spent years of therapy coming to terms with the need for separation, learning not to be a "grasping Jewish mother"—one of the hardest things I ever did. But still, how painful this pull between motherhood and autonomy, connection and self-absorption.

My ideal: that in a few years, when both my sons are full-fledged young men, I will relate to them as freestanding individuals, deeply beloved but independent; and that they will think of me the same way. A fantasy, clearly: Does any mother have that kind of uncomplicated love for her children, a love with no knots in it? Does any son think of his mother as a "freestanding individual" rather than as "Mom," sometimes loved, sometimes hated, but never truly out of his system (or his hair)?

WEDNESDAY, APRIL 21

A real spring day, the first one—blue sky, bright sun, no cold edge to the air. In the late afternoon, I walked across the Chain Bridge and down the Danube bank to the Petöfi statue; people were strolling on the bank or sitting in the metal armchairs facing the river. I saw András sitting on a bench, conversing with a friend he introduced as a former classmate from high school. Small town, Budapest. I wish the weather had been like this when Danny was here.

An editorial in *Magyar Nemzet* today drew a parallel between what's going on in Bosnia now, especially the fall of Srebrenica this week, and the fall of the Warsaw ghetto whose fiftieth anniversary was three days ago. "Waiting for Clinton" was the title of the piece, which called on the United States to do something—not to stand by and repeat the indifference of fifty years ago. I have the curious impression of watching a film being run backward. We seem to be in a situation that resembles the period right after the war, when America appeared as the world's "savior." Will it live up to the role? I'm grappling with why we should care about Srebrenica in the essay I've been writing for a public lecture at the Collegium.

Budapest Diary

Two days ago I went to an afternoon of film screenings arranged by Frances, who's pursuing her project on Hungarian cinema. I hadn't seen her since we went to Gothár's *This Day Is a Gift* together, but we've talked on the phone. The program consisted of two films, with both filmmakers present. The older work, made in the 1970s, was a famous documentary by Pál Schiffer, about a young gypsy who decides to leave his settlement in the country and come to Budapest to find work. A very gripping, moving film that one has difficulty believing was not scripted. Schiffer said during the discussion period that all the dialogue was natural and no scenes were prearranged; but there must have been a lot of editing to achieve that degree of tightness and dramatic shape.

The protagonist, whose name is the film's title (*Cséplö Gyuri*) is a good-looking, slightly built, extremely engaging young man. The film follows him and records his life over a period of several months: he works in a brick factory in the suburbs, then as a mason in the city, and lives in desolate workers' dormitories, very much alone. Finally he meets some fellow gypsies, but even then he feels lonely. He goes back to his settlement and is received with open arms, but at the end he's on the road again to Budapest. A last tragic touch is that Cséplö died about two years after the film was made, close to twenty years ago. "He turned out to have a rare heart disease and might have survived if he had gotten better medical care," Schiffer said. "But poor gypsies like him don't get that kind of care, and they didn't get it under Communism either." Several people have told me that gypsies are "Hungary's blacks," with problems very similar to those of our own black ghettos. That may have been one reason Frances, who teaches in the American studies department, chose this film.

Schiffer explained that the film was a new departure for him. Before, he had made "thematic documentaries" about social problems, including gypsies. But although they were great for discussions, he discovered they didn't *move* people—so he decided to make narrative documentaries instead, where he would follow a single individual. I'd say he discovered the power of great realist fiction—this film had some of the bittersweet qualities of great fiction films about young men and their difficulties in growing up, like Fellini's *I Vitelloni* or Olmi's *A Distant Trumpet*. Realist films are about lifelike characters, played by actors; here the character was not merely lifelike, he was real, playing himself.

I was amused by the contrast between Schiffer's film, which was factual but had the qualities of fiction, and the next one, *Gönczi the Rememberer,* a fiction film that tries to look like an unsuccessful documentary. This film is also about a gypsy, old man Gönczi, but it refuses to tell a continuous story. Gönczi is trying desperately to remember a woman's face, to see it again in his mind's eye. As it happens, some doctors have invented a machine that records on a screen what a person is seeing, whether in imagination or memory or in actuality. So Gönczi goes around for weeks followed by a camera crew, trying to recall that face; but most of the time all that's captured on screen is the grass he sees as he walks around near his hut.

"There's nothing to remember; that was my idea," said the director afterward. *Gönczi* is the work of a very young woman, Julia Szederkényi, who won a prize with it this year. She said her idea was to show that life stories are never clear and people almost never understand each other. She laughed very cheerfully while saying it!

What does it mean for young people today to think there's nothing to remember? This region of Europe is so full of reminders of historical atrocities and tragedies, it's no wonder people would rather not remember. But can they really forget? And if so, are they condemned to repeat the past, as Santayana said?

MONDAY, APRIL 26

Marvelous Sunday yesterday. After a morning working at home, I met András and we took the suburban train out to Szentendre. Gorgeous sunny day; the little village was full of strollers. The atmosphere was almost that of a Tuscan hill town, bustling central piazza, church, café terrace, relaxed people. We bumped into my American friend Stephen, who introduced us to an American friend of his named Dave: about fifty, pleasant, rugged face with a four-day stubble, wide-brimmed hat. He taught popular culture in a community college in Oregon for twenty-five years, then two years ago took advantage of an early retirement plan and came to Europe. This guy, among others I've met here, confirmed my sense that Budapest today is like Paris in the 1950s: a place where slightly oddball Americans, refusing (or having missed) the fast train to success, come to spend a few years because the living is cheap and it's far from home. Stephen himself fits the mold, being an expatriate academic and poet who came to spend a year almost two years ago and is still here with no plans to depart.

András and I walked up to the square at the top of the village, from where you can see all the rooftops and three or four churches. "Szentendre is a town of artists and churches," András commented in his best tour guide mode. He should have added, "and tourists." Sure enough, whom should we meet, standing on a parapet overlooking the town, taking photographs? Frances and her visiting friend from Los Angeles, who practically killed himself trying to get the best shot of a church steeple. We all came back on the train together, in time to see one of the subtitled Hungarian films at the BEM movie house: *The House under the Rocks*, by Károly Makk, made in the early 1950s. It's an austere, beautifully photographed black-and-white film, a naturalistic tale in which simple human beings longing for simple human happiness are thwarted by circumstances, or call it fate. The story takes place right after the war, in a poor village on the shore of Lake Balaton, and involves a love triangle: happy and beautiful married couple, unhappy hunchbacked woman who loves the man and does all she can to thwart their love. Naturally, or naturalistically, the story ends badly: the man pushes the hunchback off a cliff then confesses to his wife, even though everybody thinks it was an accident. The wife is horrified; he leaves. The end.

Interesting, how certain quasi-mythical stories are recognizable anywhere. This tale of female rivalry and thwarted passions could just as well be African or Oriental or South American as Hungarian. At the same time, one could interpret the film as a comment on the housing shortage in Hungary after the war! If the loving couple had had some privacy, the tragedy could have been averted. Or is that too simplistic? My point is, both ways of looking at it are possible—the very specific one for a particular context, and the general "universal" one transcending boundaries of time and space.

After the film we went for a drink to the jazz bar across Margit Bridge with a few other people. One was a man named Ernie, the Budapest correspondent for an American paper—a "Paris circa 1950" type. He told me he left New York fourteen years ago for what he thought would be a year; he has lived in London and Geneva, and in Budapest since 1989. I asked him how it felt to be away from home so long. "At first you think it's just for a while, then you realize it's your life," he replied.

Budapest Diary

I've been reading a book I found in a used bookstore in Szentendre, a leather-bound volume of József Kiss's collected poems published in 1900. Kiss was one of the first Jews to become a popular Hungarian author, a few years before major Jewish writers like Frigyes Karinthy or Ferenc Molnár arrived on the scene (information courtesy of András, who of course knew all about him). Leafing through the book in the store, I remembered a poem Mother had mentioned so often over the years that I couldn't possibly forget it—about a young man whose cruel sweetheart asks him to kill his mother and bring her the mother's heart. He does as she asks and is carrying the heart to her when he stumbles on the road and drops it. The heart rolls into the dust and cries out to him, "Did you hurt yourself, my son?" That pretty much gives the measure of József Kiss! But not all his poems are so cloying. Besides, Mother cited it for its content, not for its poetic value. "A mother's heart, that's what it is," she would say. Indeed, the poem is titled "The Mother's Heart" ("Az Anyaszív").

Near it is another poem, "I Would Stop beneath Your Window" ("Megállnék az ablakod alatt")—but he can't stop because it's forbidden, presumably because the lady is married. For some reason this makes me think of Mother's first love, Ernö Farkas, to whom she was "forbidden"— not because she was married, but because she was poor. He used to sing a song for her, which must have been popular at the time: "At your wedding I too will be there," obviously sung by an unhappy suitor. It must have been heartbreaking for her. I had the distinct impression, when she told me about Ernö Farkas after Daddy died, that she still mourned her first lost love.

Now there's a story about circumstances. "The girl has

no dowry, there will be no marriage," Ernö's parents must have told him: no ifs, ands, or buts. Mind you, that's exactly what Daddy's father would have said as well, had he known about his romance with Lili, but Daddy went ahead and married her anyway. Old Ernö was too obedient a son, or too much of a coward. Or not enough in love. Mother would deny that: "Oh, he was in love all right; never did marry. He had a weak character, poor man, didn't know how to put up a fight. The proof is, he didn't survive the war." Ernö and his parents died at Auschwitz. "Like sheep to the slaughter," Mother said.

Or like my uncle Izsó, who was too good to survive forced labor. "If only he had known how to take care of himself," his brother Lester would say years later. "It was harsh out there; you had to know how to keep warm, how to trade for food or an extra blanket. Izsó must have let them take everything from him, without putting up a fight. He was too good." Why do some people know how to put up a fight, while others go, docile, straight into death? And at what point does putting up a fight cross the line between self-preservation and evil? If I take the other man's blanket, I'll survive but he'll freeze to death. Who is to pass judgment on that question?

A final, more upbeat thought: By marrying for a second time when she was close to seventy, Mother realized her girlhood dream and became, for a few years at least, Mrs. Farkas. Julius Farkas is no relation to Ernö Farkas, but there's something extremely poetic, as well as ironic, in the fact that this late love had the same family name as Mother's first love, "the love of her life."

WEDNESDAY, APRIL 28

Tibor gave his public lecture at the Collegium this evening, on problems of Jewish identity in Hungary. A number of outside guests came, and there was an intense discussion afterward. Tibor is optimistic: "We are now in the same 'open' situation as Western Europe as far as Jewish options are concerned," he concluded. "Yes, there's anti-Semitism, and it's not prohibited from being voiced—that's the price to pay for the new open society." Curious how Tibor, the most cynical of men, is always hopeful where Jews in Hungary are concerned.

Farkas commented that for someone in his generation, who lived through the Holocaust and then through forty years of "repressed anti-Semitism," it's a dramatic thing to open a newspaper and read anti-Semitic statements in black and white. Tibor assured him that the followers of Csurka in Hungary today don't outnumber the followers of Le Pen in France—about 14 percent of the electorate. But Farkas pointed out that it's like unemployment: the Hungarian rate is no worse than those of Western European countries, but for a population that was used to full employment, it feels shockingly high. A sociologist reported he had just conducted a nationwide study of university students, with the following results: 5 percent were staunchly anti-Semitic, another 15–20 percent held strongly stereotyped views about Jews, and 50 percent were completely free of such stereotypes. I doubt we would do any better in the United States.

I walked all the way home after dinner, with András and a man who works in public opinion research. It was a beautiful evening, mild with a clear sky; we walked along the Danube, past the Gellért, then up Bartók Béla Avenue. The two men talked about contemporary social problems in Hungary while I listened. In one way I feel very close to all this, very involved; in another I know I'm no more than an interested observer, like an anthropologist among the natives. Care as I may, these are not my problems. Maybe that's why I could take such pleasure in the warm night air, the sound of our steps on the pavement, the stars above.

At home I found a long letter from Julie, who is back in Toronto—she enclosed a photo from one of our outings. "I'm so glad we met," she writes, "it's rare to make new friends at our age." I feel very fond of her, as I do of Robert, Farkas, Stani, Tibor, and Anna—it's truly a boon, to meet so many wonderful people in such a short time. I think it's linked to being "far from home." I'm much more available, open to new emotional ties, and so are the other temporary exiles here.

Someone like Eva, of course, is not an exile in Budapest, and she and I have become good friends too. Is it because she's very like what I might have become if I had stayed in Hungary? French professor, married with children. But would that have been an option for me, in fact? My mind boggles, trying to imagine all the unrealized possibilities.

THURSDAY, APRIL 29

Saw an outstanding production of Gogol's *The Inspector General* at the Katona József Theater tonight, with András. He convinced me I had to see it, even though I had planned to go to the movies instead. "This is world-class theater, and tomorrow is the last performance of the season," he told me on the phone yesterday. "You can see the film on video, but this is unique. You must go, I insist." So I went. There were only standing room tickets left, but we eventually found seats.

András is right; this troupe and this production are world famous. My friend Ellie, who knows about such things, wrote me about them just last week from New York. The actors are extraordinary, playing their bodies like subtle instruments, able to vary their voices from normal to hysterically high or low. They performed the play at a manic pitch, whose effect varied from boulevard farce to bitter comedy. This play is a good vehicle for that, and one can also see why it would appeal to dissidents under Communism (it's been in the repertory for over a decade): the young scoundrel who's mistaken for a government inspector plays his advantage to the hilt, while the town bureaucrats fall all over themselves trying to please him.

Afterward we walked down toward the Elizabeth Bridge and András pointed out many things I hadn't noticed—for example, the remains of a Roman wall on the square next to the Petöfi statue. "This is where the wild began, the land of the barbarians," he gestured. "Buda was the West, Pest was the barbaric East. And that's how the division will fall economically too, the western versus the eastern part of the Danube; you'll see." Today, of course, Budapest as a whole is "west of the Danube." András's East-West division reminded me of what Tibor said in one of our first Collegium discussions about "eastern" versus "western" Central Europe. These binary divisions die hard, if at all.

Again I had proof of András's enormous love for this city—he has obviously studied every nook and cranny. "That's why I never left," he said, when I expressed my admiration. "I'd be miserable living anywhere else." He lives in that neighborhood, a few blocks from the bridge. "My father said I should invite you, but we live like real bachelors—I must give the place a good cleaning before I can ask you there," he said. His father is eighty-nine, and after spending the winter inside he has started to go out again. He's *csavarog* again, said András. *Csavarogni*, such an expressive verb—it means both hanging out doing nothing in particular and walking around looking for adventure. Like French *flâner*.

András's mother was his father's second wife—his first wife and two daughters were killed at Auschwitz, along with many other members of the family. András is the only child of Holocaust survivors, like my brother-in-law, Sam. András's mother, unmarried at the time, was deported to Ravensbrück; she met and married his father after the war. She was a children's dressmaker and did very good business before the war; afterward she was a broken woman, "physically, spiritually, psychologically," András said. That was the woman he knew, since he was born after the war. She died about fifteen years ago.

SATURDAY, MAY 1

I met Stani and András this morning to go to the May Day festivities in City Park. The two men were already there when I got off the bus at Heroes' Square—one big and paunchy, the other much shorter and thinner, talking animatedly. I suddenly felt very fond of them, seeing them like that in the midst of strangers, gesticulating in the sunlight.

City Park was full of people, a carnival atmosphere with food and drink, stands selling stuffed animals, clothes, cotton candy. Taped rock music blared from a loudspeaker, but the live action was all seriously political: a to-do organized by the Socialist Party, formerly the Communists, with representatives from Romania, Germany, and Italy. The speakers were all together on a podium at the edge of a large grassy plot. Among the topics they discussed were unemployment and privatization. The Socialist leader, Gyula Horn, said they're not against privatization, just against the way it's being implemented: too many people are falling by the wayside on the road to the free market.

We stood on the grass watching the speakers, but the sun was blazing hot; after a few minutes we walked back to Heroes' Square, where Stani took the subway. András and I stayed and had lunch on the terrace at the edge of the park.

András could be quite attractive if he were thinner; some well-cut clothes would also do wonders. He told me he met a woman from Latvia fifteen years ago, when he was a tour guide (that's why he knows Budapest so well—he was a guide during the summers in his student days), who still writes to him and sends him photos and wants to marry him.

"It's just because she wants to come to Budapest. I don't have any illusions about her loving me," he said. But maybe she does, he admitted. Still, he's afraid to ask her to come here because she would never leave, and what would he do with her?

"Why don't you go visit her?" I asked.

"There's no point. I'm sure she'd want a child, and I can't afford that. I adore Marika [his daughter], but couldn't support another child. Believe me, I've thought it over."

He has pretty much resigned himself to not having a sexual relationship with a woman: "I don't live alone, and the apartment consists of two adjoining rooms."

"Have you ever thought of leaving?"

"Yes, I had the chance several times. But my parents were old, and they had no one besides me. I couldn't leave them." His mother was forty when he was born, his father forty-four. A very Eastern European story.

On the way to the subway he pointed out the Yugoslav embassy on the corner of Andrássy Avenue. "That's where poor Imre Nagy took refuge in 1956." Then he told me the whole story: The police got Nagy and his friends to surrender, promising they could go home. But the Russians took over the bus and drove them all to Romania, including the women and children. From there Nagy and the other men were brought back to jail in Budapest, tried, and hanged.

On the edge of the park, András showed me a tree-lined area where the colossal statue of Stalin once stood, on top of the reviewing stand used by Party officials on May Day and other holidays. That was the statue the rebels toppled in 1956, then dispersed piece by piece over the following days. "But the reviewing stand remained, and a somewhat smaller statue of Lenin was put up at one side of it that same year," András said. The Lenin statue is now with all the other Communist monuments, in the park of discarded statues that's due to open soon.

SUNDAY, JUNE 6

Returned to Budapest this morning after a week in Holland and three weeks in the States. Michael has moved back East, much to my relief. I prolonged my stay to spend time with him in Princeton.

I'm still jet-lagged and slightly disoriented; the heat doesn't help, heavy, humid summer weather that cools off in the evening but is extremely oppressive during the day.

I have the feeling of a *fin de régime*, as if the days were numbered until my final departure. Sitting on the bus to-day, I told myself I'd have to start making lists. I could see myself crossing out the items one by one: visit the top of Mount Gellért, the ethnographic museum, the Museum of Decorative Arts; get a copy of my birth certificate; visit the Orthodox cemetery; investigate the death of Grandfather Stern; go to Nyíregyháza to get Mother's birth certificate, make the trip to Daddy's birthplace, Gorlice. More than I can chew, very likely. I've simply got to finish my work by the end of this month, to have a bit of time to play.

MONDAY, JUNE 7

A moth is climbing up the computer screen as I write. There are no screens on the windows in the apartment, and naturally the bugs come to the light. Doesn't anyone ever open the window here in summer, or are they used to having the bugs come? Today we had two big thundershowers, and the air feels a bit less heavy. But it's still too humid out, oppressive.

Late dinner with Katalin, one of my young Hungarian friends from Cambridge, home for the summer. Among other things, we spoke about the relation between women and men in Hungary. Katalin has strong views on that. "Here a brilliant woman counts only if her name is associated with an even more brilliant man. With very few exceptions, women don't make their reputation by forging their own way—it's always by 'whose girlfriend she is, or was' that people judge a woman. And when a brilliant woman marries a man less intelligent or successful than she is, people find it strange, incomprehensible."

She grew quite indignant as she talked, as if this were true only of Hungary. Sounds pretty familiar to me. (Obviously, this description doesn't fit all cases—either here or elsewhere, I assume.)

I called András when I got home—it was really good to talk to him. I can't figure out just what our relationship is: good friends, confidants (he likes to speak about "amorous adventures" without giving any details), or is there something more? "Between a man and a woman, there's always some weakness on one side that makes things difficult," he said tonight, and I couldn't help thinking it had some reference to him and me. At any rate, I find him extremely witty and fun. I actually missed him, a little, while I was in the States.

TUESDAY, JUNE 8

Dinner at the Tabáni Kakas, with a Collegium group after the panel discussion organized by Robert—a big, noisy, high-spirited crowd. Robert's girlfriend was there; they were cooing at each other, very much in love.

One of Robert's guests, the conservative Englishman Edward, sat next to me. He holds himself very stiffly, as if he were in the saddle, exaggerating the posture of the perfect horseman. He drank an enormous quantity of wine.

"People are always trying to restrain me," he said.

"What if someone told you, 'Go ahead and take your pleasure.' What would you do?" I asked him.

"Oh, I'd probably collapse."

THURSDAY, JUNE 10

I gave my lecture at the Collegium this evening: "The Politics of Postmodernism after the Wall, or What Do We Do When the Ethnic Cleansing Starts?" This will be the last chapter of my book, I've decided. It's very much a product of my time and thinking in Budapest. The only political question I care about, finally, is how to prevent people from committing murder, in the name of whatever ideology or religion or group identity or fear one cares to name.

I was pleased to see how many of the Hungarians I had invited came to the lecture. Eva, Aniko, and Ilona (the philosophy professor, whom I've seen a few times) were pretty much sure bets, but not the others; I also had the pleasant surprise of seeing again my friend István, whom I met at an international conference in Tokyo two years ago. He's been teaching in the States but is back home for the summer. I have very warm feelings toward István, because he was the one who put me in touch with János, with Eva, and with several others I met during my first weeks here. In addition, there were a few people I didn't know who turned out to be interesting, including a young sociologist who has written about postmodernism and was excited about the talk. The dear rector positively beamed, like a proud parent at his child's performance.

Budapest Diary

This evening, concert at the Bartók house, up on a hill in Buda. It's the house where Bartók lived from 1932 to 1940, when he moved to New York to protest Hungary's alliance with the Nazis. He was by then world famous, very respected in Hungary, and—most important for the time—not Jewish, so he could have stayed without any problem.

The house is now a museum, with a small exhibition showing his workroom and the books he had in his personal library (he read Flaubert in French, Dickens in English). A wall display highlights the main facts of his life. I was particularly impressed by a letter he wrote to another Hungarian in the States in 1942, when he became president of an anti-Nazi émigré organization: "It is our duty as Hungarian intellectuals to represent to the world the other side of Hungary, which doesn't support the Nazis." In June 1945, after the defeat, he sent out new letters asking for contributions to the relief effort in Hungary, where people lacked food and other necessities. Later that year he died of blood cancer.

It's rare to see artistic genius so beautifully wedded to ordinary human decency.

The concert was wonderful, works for piano and violin by Bartók and Ravel, performed by two young musicians. Ilona had organized the outing for some of the Fulbrights from the university and had invited me along.

MONDAY, JUNE 14

Feel good today, after an honest day's work. I gave my seminar on American feminist criticism at the Institute of Literary Studies this morning, at Eva's invitation. I spoke in English, with a young colleague from the Institute acting as translator. Not exactly an overflow crowd, and only five men present, but that's not too bad considering this is work in the trenches. Afterward the translator introduced me to a woman who edits one of the Institute's journals. She wants to publish some excerpts from my book *Subversive Intent*, which he offered to translate.

To be a published author in Hungarian! If only Mother could have lived to see this. Not to mention Daddy.

After the seminar I had lunch with Eva in a small restaurant nearby. Her grandfather, she told me, was mayor of Budapest from 1937 to 1942—a man of the right, but not a fascist. He resigned in 1942, well before the Nazis entered Hungary.

"I had trouble getting admitted to the university, carrying that name—not so much because he was right wing, but because he was a 'class enemy,'" she said. She had a chance to change her name when she married, but she's stubborn and retained her maiden name, as is the custom here among professional women. When she first started working at the Institute, as a lowly bilingual secretary despite her diplomas, the culture minister Aczél wrote to the head of the Institute: "What are names like K. and S. doing in that institution?" K. is Eva's name, and S. is that of a well-known professor who was just starting out then and came from an aristocratic family. "Good old Communist eyes; no one escapes them, not even a lowly secretary," Eva commented.

TUESDAY, JUNE 15

Ellen, my artist friend, arrived from New Haven today for a two-week visit. I think she'll enjoy it. She loves to walk around cities, and she has a sharp visual relation to things and an eye for detail I've noticed only among artists. She plans to photograph all the interesting buildings to show to her husband, an architect.

This morning, before Ellen arrived, I went to the Institute of Literary Studies to attend the Hungarian ritual known as the *kandidátusi* something or other, a public thesis defense like the French *défense de thèse*. Here it's even more formal than in France: there are seven jury members and two "public opponents" who have written up their opinions so the candidate can reply to them. The candidate this morning was István, my friend from Tokyo. In the audience I noticed Aniko and several other people I recognized, including a few who had attended my seminar yesterday. I sat next to Eva, who filled me in on the more esoteric details. She said István's thesis is brilliant and everybody knows it, but it also irritates many people because he attacks all the specialists in the field. Several members of the jury (all male) faulted him for his sarcastic style and his scorn for his predecessors. The two harshest ones accused him of shabby scholarship, of not citing some indispensable works. I leaned over and whispered to Eva: "If this is what they do to a brilliant thesis, what do they say about the mediocre ones?"

"Oh, nothing—those just sail through," she answered.

This evening Ellen and I went to a concert at the Music Academy, and I bumped into someone from the Institute, who told me that in the end all went well for István. I saw Tibor and his daughter visiting from Paris, as well as a Hungarian woman who had come to one of the Collegium lectures and a visiting American acquaintance from Boston. Budapest is beginning to feel more and more like a hometown.

THURSDAY, JUNE 17

Just got back from dinner at the home of Ádám, a well-known professor I had met abroad on various occasions. He lives with his wife and two daughters in a grand house that once belonged to his family but was nationalized in

1952. They are thus tenants in what would rightfully be their own house. The place is full of beautiful period furniture in polished woods; floor-to-ceiling bookcases line the walls of the living room and dining room, and there are paintings everywhere. The family boasts several famous painters, besides a number of minor ones. Ádám showed me these treasures almost reluctantly and with a kind of ironic laugh, saying several times: "Well, let's leave all this." I had to insist that the works really interested me, and his wife (a folklorist who knows Anna) also had to push him a little. He finally gave me the full tour, including his daughters' rooms, their walls crammed with beautiful drawings and paintings.

After dinner we sat in the living room, and just when I began to make moves to leave, the conversation turned to Hungarian literary journals and Hungarian literature. Ádám began to take down from his shelves copies of half a dozen journals, including one he edits, as well as several dictionaries of Hungarian literature to which he had contributed. He showed me an autographed copy of a fat book by Péter Esterházy, a difficult "postmodern" novelist who is probably the most respected writer in Hungary today and whose work Ádám was one of the first to promote. Ádám is obviously a passionate and erudite reader of Hungarian literature, and I think he would have been happy to spend several more hours talking about it. When I finally left, it was close to midnight.

This visit has given me a much more positive image of Ádám. When one meets him at a formal gathering or a conference, he appears cold and even arrogant. But my new impression is that these are cover-ups for a deep well of reserve and shyness. He too has the sardonic manner of the Central European intellectual (similar in feeling to Tibor's, though not identical in form), and in his case one additional reason might be that his family lost so much during the

Communist regime. He told me he was even denied entry into the university until his mother pleaded with one of his father's old friends who had become a big cheese in the Party. A few incidents of that kind will do wonders for one's sense of irony.

SATURDAY, JUNE 19—PÉCS

Ellen and I are on a weekend outing. Danny will be amused to hear that we drove here in a Lada, a white tin box. It was the cheapest rental, and it runs just fine.

Pécs is a beautiful city, about a three-hour drive from Budapest, home of the Zsolnay porcelain museum among many others; it has a good university and is also the city where one can see most of the works of K. Tivadar Csontváry, a mad modernist painter who was one of Hungary's greatest artists. We'll visit the museums tomorrow. Right now I'm sitting on a bed in our room in the Hotel Palatinus, a few steps from the magnificent central square, which is bounded by ornate gelato-colored buildings; at one end of the square sits the huge, squat mosque-turned-Catholic-church, built of bricks. The Turks left mosques and minarets behind in many cities after they were driven out in 1680.

We visited the synagogue this afternoon, soon after we arrived here—I had noticed the Star of David on the map and wondered what we would find. The synagogue is near the city center, at one end of another nice square; built in the baroque mode like many churches around here, but without a bell tower and with Hebrew letters and the Ten Commandments decorating the facade. Inside, it's decorated like a church: beautiful painted ceiling (flower motifs, as in the Mátyás Church) and carved oak galleries where the women used to sit. The synagogue was built between

1865 and 1869, at the beginning of the great flowering of Jewish presence in Hungary.

Before the war the Jews in Pécs numbered 4,000; after the war, about 400. They were deported on July 4, 1944, just a few days before the deportations stopped because Admiral Miklós Horthy (Hungary's authoritarian leader since the 1920s) refused to sign any more orders. I've heard some people praise Horthy for this, forgetting that he had signed a great many orders during the preceding months. The elderly man who sold us our entry tickets told us about the deportation, then added: "Just think, if they had waited a few days longer . . ." But they didn't wait, and so 90 percent of the Jews of Pécs disappeared. There will be a memorial service on July 4, performed every year, at which they will open the "Book of Tears" and read the names of all the people who perished.

"Is the subject of conversation usually the Jews, or is it just because of us?" Ellen asked yesterday, as we left the party one of István's friends gave to celebrate his successful thesis. Before we left, Ellen got into a discussion with Aniko's husband, Peter, and an older man named Zoltán, who used to be Peter's professor (both men are married to women "of Jewish origin"). Peter claimed, Ellen reported, that it's dangerous to be a Jew in Hungary.

"When?" she asked. "The 1930s, the 1940s, or do you mean now?"

"Always," he answered.

SUNDAY, JUNE 20

Back from our trip, tired but satisfied. I drove from Pécs, since Ellen had driven there. We went to Mohács, a sleepy town on the Danube, where the Turks fought their decisive victory over the Hungarians in 1526, inaugurating their 160 year rule. The Battle of Mohács appears to be the only interesting thing about Mohács, so we turned around and drove to Kecskemét, where we arrived just as the sun was setting. Wonderful park in the middle of the city, with many people out strolling. Three churches and an extremely ambitious city hall are all squeezed together very picturesquely on Kossuth Lajos Square. The poet Petöfi went to school here, we learned from one of the inscriptions. My favorite buildings were at the other end of the park, facing each other: a former synagogue (now used as an office building, the guidebook says) that had a truly strange cupola, like a dark pear perched on top of a tower rising from the middle; and an art nouveau extravaganza with crazy curved stucco, inlaid Zsolnay tiles, and large colorful designs on the facade, probably of ceramic tile as well. The whole thing gave a wildly eccentric impression, but I loved it. It's called the Cziffra Palota, the Fancy Palace.

MONDAY, JUNE 21

Richard Rorty, the American philosopher, spoke at the Collegium this evening to a full house. He is very well known in Europe, I've noticed, with many of his works published in translation. He said pretty much what I thought he'd say, speaking against universalism (no such thing as universal truth) but for democracy (we have to do what we can). He strikes me as approachable, modest, and very American. Among the Hungarians in the audience were the philosophers Agnes Heller and her husband Ferenc Fehér, who both teach in the States. She asked a very long question, almost a minilecture; she appears to be someone who's absolutely certain of her own opinions.

At the reception after the lecture, I saw Ádám and Tibor deep in conversation in one corner, so I went over and joined them. They were talking about a publishing incident involving the journal Ádám edits. A man had sent in a memoir about the war, in which he told how some of the rich Jews in Budapest struck a deal directly with Joseph Goebbels to enable them to leave Hungary in 1944. Furthermore, he claimed that some of the lucky ones actually crossed a few other Jewish names off the list on the grounds that "they didn't belong," that is, weren't rich enough or high-class enough to be saved—which, if true, would be truly shocking. Ádám showed the manuscript to his aunt, who has firsthand knowledge of that incident; she protested and asked him to edit out a few sentences, which he did; he then published the text. Naturally the author's furious to have been edited like that without his permission. He has sent in yet another memoir, this time "telling all," even things he himself had edited out earlier.

"What will you do?" I asked.

"I'm checking out his claims, and then we'll see."

In a curious way, I had the impression that he and Tibor took pleasure in these awful stories about the heartlessness and egotism of upper-class Jews, but I may have been imagining it. Some of those Jews were still harboring a grudge against the 1919 Kun regime, according to Ádám: "They blamed the Horthy regime's anti-Semitism on Kun. 'If we had 1944, it was all because of 1919,' they'd say." A case of class interest taking precedence over religious or ethnic solidarity, a Marxist might say.

In any case, it's not a pretty story.

WEDNESDAY, JUNE 23

Fascinating dinner at Aniko and Peter's house last night. István and his wife were there, as well as Nándor, a visiting émigré from New York, and Peter's old professor Zoltán and his wife. At first the conversation was slow, especially as people felt obliged to speak English because of Ellen.

After several hours of desultory talk, already quite late in the evening, I threw out the question: "Are you sorry the old regime is gone?" Zoltán, a large, mustached fellow, a professor of literature at the university and a very sardonic, witty man, replied immediately: "You bet I am!" There followed two hours of deeply engaged discussion, in Hungarian (I translated), about the pros and cons of the Kádár regime.

"You understand, everyone knew it was a joke—Kádár himself considered it a joke. But it worked, and people laughed a lot. Now, everyone's serious—and they're right, there's nothing to laugh about," Zoltán said.

Peter protested, though not very strongly, that in the old days one was often harassed when leaving the country, and it was not well looked upon to read the Western press (available at places like the British Council).

"Yeah, well, just try taking down the chaplain's posters at the university, and then we'll talk. I'm scared!" said Zoltán. In his view there's a new repression that's even worse than the old one, because no one really believed in the proclaimed values of the old regime whereas the neonationalists and the neoreligious people are serious. "There aren't even any good jokes anymore," Zoltán concluded.

István, who kept nodding his head, then told a joke he had heard recently—the only one he'd heard recently, he said. It was a Jewish joke: "Cohn and Grün meet in the street, and Cohn looks very prosperous: new suit, expensive shoes, a foreign car at his disposal. Grün says to him, 'What happened to you? Only last week, you were walking around in rags!' Cohn replies: 'Remember the Christian family who hid me during the war, who saved my life? Well, I'm blackmailing them.'"

Everyone burst out laughing, getting it immediately: nowadays Christians who helped Jews during the war have something to hide rather than something to be proud of. "That's about as dark a piece of humor as one is likely to get," I remarked. Zoltán, smiling broadly, announced: "I put that joke into circulation a couple of months ago."

"It's pretty terrible," I said.

"Yeah, well, things are pretty terrible," he replied.

István's wife, Ági, a linguist, is less pessimistic: "Let's wait until the elections. I can't believe people will vote for the extreme right."

"We had hoped for something very different," István said. "No one among us foresaw this wave of nationalism." He's a very gentle, quiet man who doesn't speak much, but I find him extremely thoughtful and appealing.

Zoltán, a completely different type, told a hilarious story about the drunken young man who said to him in a bar last week, "I'll die for my Hungarian homeland!" The way he imitated the drunk, insisting especially on the word *haza*, "homeland," made all of us double up with laughter. "No one would ever have said such an idiotic thing under the old regime," Zoltán commented.

And democracy? I asked. Everyone shrugged their shoulders. "Democracy? When was there any form of democracy in this country? Before the war, it was Horthy; and before that, 'Austrian liberalism'—and before that. . . . You were too young when you left this country," Nándor said (he had been quiet most of the evening). "If you had been ten years older, you would know better."

The curious thing is that all these people are doing very nicely under the new regime: their pay's not great, but they manage to cobble together several positions, each with its own salary, or else one member of a couple earns more in the private sector, like Aniko. They have all traveled and studied abroad in the past few years, received fellowships, participated in exchange programs. Maybe their pessimism is just part of the famous "Hungarian melancholy." As several people have told me, both the divorce rate and the suicide rate in Hungary are among the highest in the world.

It will be interesting indeed to see how the elections turn out next spring.

Enormous Changes at the Last Minute

Back from the conference in Spain, back home in Buda-pest. In a little over three weeks, it'll be a more lasting good-bye. I'm already feeling sad about that.

The man next to me on the plane this morning, a chemi-cal engineer who teaches at the university, mentioned the inflation of 1946, when his mother went out to buy a bus pass that cost 3,000,000 pengös; only by the time she got there, the price had gone up to 3,200,000. A young man gave her the extra money, "and she still owes it to him," my neighbor said. This story came about because I gave him 5 pesetas to complete his purchase of some duty-free cognac. It's less than a dime, I assured him—not to worry. "I'll be like my mother, who still owes a man 200,000 pengös he gave her in 1946," he said with a laugh, and told me the story.

Last week at the Ecseri flea market, I bought some bills from those years: a 1,000 pengö note with the bust of a lady wearing roses in her hair; a 100,000 pengö note with a pretty girl dressed in a folk dress, a braid down her back; and a 1,000,000 pengö note with a portrait of Lajos Kos-suth, the hero of 1848. The first two bills are from 1945, the third from 1946—a perfect illustration of the inflation. I paid about 20 forints apiece for them. It's strange to think these were the bills Mother and Daddy handled after the war. I had completely forgotten (if I ever knew it) that the postwar money was still the pengö, not the forint.

People are worried about inflation now too, but it's mild compared with 1946. The price of my monthly bus pass has gone up by about 15 percent since February.

Big news about Csurka: he was a police informer under the Kádár regime! Frances told me over the phone this afternoon. The news broke while I was in Spain, so I hadn't heard about it. In his column in this week's *Magyar Forum*, Csurka explains he was forced to do it and says he never gave any valuable information, never "sold" anybody—which is highly doubtful, because he couldn't have gotten away with not providing any information for so many years.

This confirms what some people have told me about his Communist past (one person said he had "toadied" to the Communists in the 1950s). Curiously, though, the revelation doesn't seem to have tarnished his popularity among the readers of *Magyar Forum*. The right-wing nationalists still love him. In fact he has founded his own party after having been ousted from the MDF. "About time they ousted him," the rector said to me the other day. "He's been a liability, making the MDF seem more right-wing than it is, on the whole. But they waited too long; they should have condemned him the minute he started his anti-Semitic nonsense. They may live to regret it." That was an allusion to next year's elections.

It's none of my business, but it seems to me that if a party can lose an election because of its anti-Semitism (or what is perceived as such), that's a good thing. Too bad for the MDF if it loses, but three cheers for Hungarians.

MONDAY, JULY 5

This evening I made a point of going to see the much praised *Szindbád*, a cult film based on a famous novel by Gyula Krudy. András is always singing its praises, but from my point of view it's a dud. "Arty" to the point of tedium—no story, just a series of repetitive scenes showing the world-weary hero and the dozens of women he seduced throughout his life. I haven't read the Krudy novel, but if it's anything like the film, I wouldn't like it. The film reminded me of the one about the painter Csontváry I saw back in February, which was equally pretentious. No wonder—it was made by the same director, Zoltán Huszárik.

TUESDAY, JULY 6

Thanks to András, who gave me the exact location (35 Dob Street, one flight up) I finally went to the Orthodox Community Bureau today—to inquire about the location of the tombs of Moshe Stern and the Rubin grandparents in the Orthodox cemetery, but also to see the place where Daddy worked.

It doesn't seem to have changed much. Large foyer and front office, old furniture, dusty air. When the woman behind the desk heard I wanted grave locations, she pointed to a door on the left: "In there, they'll give you the information." I went in and saw a pleasant, intelligent-looking middle-aged man standing behind a desk. He introduced himself, I introduced myself, we shook hands.

"What can I do for you?" Mr. H. asked. I told him what I wanted, and he took down a large, ancient-looking book with handwritten entries. "Stern, Moshe Chaim. Son of Chaya Sarah. Pál utca 3. Died in 1924, age forty-five." Was he the one?

"I was under the impression he might have died earlier, around 1919," I said.

"Then he's not the one, because they didn't start burying in this cemetery until 1923." That clears up the mystery, because I know for a fact that Grandfather Stern is buried there. Milton must have confused him with another relative, or else his being killed by a "Hungary Firster" was a myth that had somehow made its way into the family. Of course he still could have been beaten in 1919, but he didn't die then. He could also have been beaten in 1924, though it's less likely.

Budapest Diary

Finding Baruch Rubin and "Mrs. Baruch Rubin (no Hebrew name known)" was much easier. He died in the spring of 1952 (the exact dates are given in Hebrew), age sixty-seven; Esther died in 1959, age seventy-five. That means he was born in 1885, she in 1884—not very usual, at the time, for a man to marry a woman a year older. (History repeats itself: Mother and Daddy, my husband and I.) Let's assume they were married in 1909, or at the earliest 1908—they wouldn't have waited more than two years to have a child, and Daddy was born in 1910. Baruch would have been twenty-three or twenty-four at the time of the marriage, Esther twenty-four or twenty-five. She was quite beautiful, according to the photos I've seen, and her family was well off; her mother ran a prosperous pub on the outskirts of Gorlice, in Galicia, a region in southeastern Poland that was heavily settled by Jews in the last century. The men in the family, being *cohens* and very religious, spent most of their time studying Talmud and left the business of day-to-day life to their wives. But I've heard from my aunt Rózsi that Esther's father was actually an astute businessman, dealing in lumber. Baruch was much poorer, the son of a humble Hebrew-school teacher; his mother died when he was a boy, and his older brother emigrated to America about the time Baruch went to Budapest. Although poor, he was good-looking and a *cohen*, which made him a desirable suitor. Might this match provide one explanation for Grandfather's outrage at Daddy's marrying a poor woman who was older than he? His own wife, though a bit older, at least came from the right kind of family (as did he).

The ancient-looking book in Mr. H.'s office has two systems of entries, one alphabetical in the back, one chronological in the front. The Stern and Rubin entries were in different books, separated by thirty years; by now, I imagine there are no more than a few entries a year, since most

Jews are buried in the Reform cemetery, whose records are kept in the Reform Community Bureau on Sip Street. Very complicated, for such a small Jewish community.

After we had dealt with the graves, I asked Mr. H. about Daddy: "My father worked in this Bureau from about 1935 until we left Hungary in 1949. Is there any chance somebody might remember him, or that there's a file on him?"

"You'll have to talk to my wife about that; she keeps all those records," he said. "Unfortunately, many of our books are missing. Too bad you can't find someone who might have known him."

"Yes. A few years ago, there was still an old gentleman around who had worked with him—my aunt gave me his phone number. But when I called in February, I got his daughter instead. He had died in November."

"Well, come back and see what my wife can find."

On my way out, I meant to look around very carefully: Are these the very rooms where Daddy lived and breathed? But in the end I hurried away.

István, on the phone tonight, asked me, "Do you think your stay here has had an impact on your work?"

"Oh, yes. The book I just finished would have been quite different if I had stayed in the States." I realized even as I was saying it how true it was. The orientation toward history, so emphasized in my new book, would have been much more muted if I had stayed at home. There my emphasis was on the "personal voice." Here I'm constantly being forced to see the personal in historical terms, as part of a collective experience.

THURSDAY, JULY 8

Dinner with Frances and her old friend Pali this evening. Pali, a historian, is interesting and friendly, and very Hungarian—about sixty, nice-looking, knows everybody among the Budapest intelligentsia and the Free Democrat politicians, most of whom are members of the intelligentsia.

We spoke at length about the *Szindbád* film, after I mentioned my disappointment of the other night. "The most beautiful Hungarian film ever made," Pali said. But he admitted it was very much "from the male point of view." "Every man, without exception, identifies with Szindbád," he affirmed, with a slight touch of irony but with real conviction. "The world-weary lover who turns to women as mother, nurse, lover—and only the most beautiful women, always beautiful, adorable women! What man could resist such an idea?"

"Oh yeah, and what about the women, don't they have a point of view?" Frances and I protested with mock indignation. But it was a lost cause. As far as I can tell, there's a cult surrounding the filmmaker Huszárik and the actor Zoltán Latinovits, as well as the writer Krudy—all heavy drinkers, great womanizers, and artists of genius; and all of them dead at a relatively early age. The whole of Huszárik's oeuvre consists of *Szindbád*, the Csontváry film I saw, plus four shorts; yet his reputation is sky high among film buffs in Hungary.

We spoke English, because of Frances. Pali speaks it very well, making just a few mistakes in pronunciation from time to time (*dinamit* for dynamite). When Frances went to the bathroom, we switched to Hungarian. "I hadn't realized you knew Hungarian," Pali had said to me early during the dinner. "How come?"

"I was born here."

"Well, that's a good reason."

But the really big news, which I'm almost afraid to write about, is my return visit to 35 Dob Street yesterday afternoon, where I had an appointment with Mrs. H. She is youngish, plump, talkative, and extremely nice. She received me in an office that was partially filled with bags of old clothes destined for Bosnia. A young boy wearing a yarmulke was sitting at a small desk, stamping hundreds of what looked like little notebooks. He reminded me of Danny—same dark good looks, about the same age. Mrs. H. later told me he's the son of a good friend who wants to "keep him off the streets" now that school is out and asked her to find him something to do. He did his busywork while listening to our conversation.

The first matter of business was Daddy, and there I'm afraid we drew a blank. The earliest records they have date from November 1949, after we left. All the others were destroyed. I wasn't quick enough to quiz her about that: things were destroyed during the war, but why afterward? The fact is, no record.

The next question was the marriage certificate, and there too we had no luck. We looked through two books for the years 1935–38, but there was no record of a religious wedding for Miklós Rubin—there was a Ferenc Rubin but not Miklós. Does that mean they weren't married at the Kazinczy Street synagogue? Very likely. Where then? "Maybe it was a small, low-key ceremony," she said. But I remember the wedding pictures—Mother's beautiful white satin dress, Daddy's frock coat and top hat. That was no small private ceremony, unless the photos lied. We agreed I'd try to find out more from my aunt Rózsi; in the meantime, another blank.

Then we hit paydirt, for she found my birth record. On the bottom half of a page, between Zuszman Robert born on July 14, 1939, and Kohn József born on September 20, was I, Rubin Zsuzsana Magdolna. Born on July 18, 1939, at 12:15 P.M.; girl; legitimate. Parents' place of marriage: Budapest 7 (the Acacia Street district). Father's Hebrew name: Yitzhak Moshe Hacohen—I never knew that "Hacohen" was part of one's name. Father's family name and profession: Rubin Isaac Moses, *hitk.* [short for *hitközségi,* referring to the Bureau] *tisztviselö:* administrator, clerk. Mother's Hebrew name: Rivka. Family name: Stern Livia.

"You told me her name was Lillian," Mrs. H. said.

"Well, everyone always called her Lili," I replied. But her real name was Livia—I wonder why it was never used. Maybe it was like my sister Judy, whose real name is Eve— but her middle name is Judy, so it's not the same. Parents' address and child's place of birth: Akácfa u. 59, Bókay u. 4. "Ah, that's the children's clinic on Bókay. There was a famous doctor there, but he didn't perform deliveries," said Mrs. H. (Now I know where to go for the "excerpt from the motherbook" of my birth certificate.) Day of the name giving: July 20, 1939. Helpful Mrs. H.: "What day was the eighteenth? Must have been a Thursday, and they gave the name on the very next Shabbos."

Could we photocopy the birth record? I asked her. Yes, of course, she said. "I'll go down with you and get it done in the place downstairs." But I wasn't quite ready to do that yet, because I had remembered something else.

"In 1946 my mother gave birth to a boy who died after a few days. Is there a chance we can find an entry for him?"

"It's doubtful, if he only lived a few days—they probably wouldn't put him in the book. Let's look." Nothing. But he would certainly be in the death registry. "My husband handles that. He takes care of the deaths; I do the living," she laughed. "Laci!" she cried loudly. From the other room, he yelled back, "What is it?"

"The lady has another person she would like to look up." So he came in, and we told him the story. He disappeared for a little while, then came back carrying a register.

"He was a day old." Down toward the bottom of the page among the other *R*s was my little brother: Rubin András, one day. No Hebrew name; he died too early. The date of death was given in Hebrew, but Mr. H. looked it up: September 1, 1946.

This morning I woke up with a sudden thought: When little András was born (August 31, 1946), I was seven years and one month old; when my son Daniel was born, his brother Michael was seven years and one month old. Uncanny coincidence—once more I have the feeling that I am repeating, with variations, Mother's life. That's why I keep thinking I'll get married again someday, or at least find another life companion. She was an "alone-standing woman" for eighteen years after Daddy died. By that standard, and even if I use 1979 as the starting point (the summer all hell broke loose), I still have four years to go before meeting my man. She married Julius when she was sixty-nine, so I'm still ahead.

Next Wednesday I will go to Nyíregyháza to get Mother's birth certificate. Maybe it will list an address for her place of birth—wouldn't that be interesting? I have the feeling of living an exciting detective story, and yet when you think about it objectively, it's a poor little story of nothing at all. But it's mine, and that makes all the difference. I do feel sad that so little, almost nothing really, remains about Daddy. When I think back to how important he seemed to me during the years I was going to school in the building where he worked, as if he were the chief director of a major enterprise, and then look around at the dusty little office that contains not a single trace or record of his ever having set foot in it, I experience a strong sense of irony—but that's probably not the right word. More a sense akin to the "Ozymandias syndrome"—desert sands covering up the broken monument of the great king Ozymandias. Or maybe it's Ecclesiastes: "Vanity, everything is vanity."

It's true that some people leave traces behind when they die. Even I will, with my books and my "memorial minute" as a Harvard professor. But being philosophical about it, one has to say it's simply a matter of scale: Miklós Rubin's traces took less time to disappear than Susan Rubin Suleiman's will. They'll both end in oblivion.

Gloomy thoughts, especially considering that today, officially, finally, I finished my book: *Risking Who One Is: Encounters with Contemporary Art and Literature*. I'm dedicating it to Judy. I kept telling people I was writing a book my sister could read, so what more appropriate dedicatee than she? Anyway, the gloomy thoughts describe only part of how I feel about tracking down the past. The other part, as I have said, is a feeling of excitement and pleasure.

SATURDAY, JULY 10

Mother sometimes mentioned the name Moritz Scharf. I learned today he was the son of one of the defendants in the famous Tiszaeszlár trial of 1882, in which two Jewish men were accused of killing a young Christian servant girl. In reality she had thrown herself into the river, but the men were accused of ritually raping and murdering her. The trial was held in Nyíregyháza, with high drama. Young Moritz was brainwashed into testifying against his father (that's what fascinated Mother, I think), but in the end justice prevailed. The two men were acquitted with the help of a Christian lawyer, a member of the prominent Eötvös family. Like the Dreyfus case in France a decade later, this one became a cause célèbre and provoked anti-Semitic riots.

András gave me the history lesson while we were driving to Györ this morning, or rather I was driving and he talked. Györ is a large city (by Hungarian standards) in the north, near the Austrian border; it has beautiful baroque houses, nice squares, and old streets. It also has a monumental Jewish synagogue, unused and boarded up. In front of the synagogue is a park, and attached to it are some other buildings that were once the Community Bureau but are now a music school. Those buildings look restored, but the synagogue itself, massive, with two asymmetrical domes and several towers, is near ruin.

If the synagogue is any indication, the Jewish population of Györ must have been very large and prosperous and proud. Compared with this, the grand synagogue of Pécs looks positively modest! Today there are almost no Jews left in Györ. András's father had a lot of family there; some were taken away during the war, others left in 1956, emigrating to Australia. Today's trip was a kind of pilgrimage for András; he hadn't been in this region for many years. "My father won't be around much longer. In a way, I'm making this trip in his place," he said after telling me about the family.

From Györ we drove to Pannonhalma, famous for its monastery and church dating to the time of Hungary's founding father Árpád, who died about A.D. 900. The complex is beautifully situated, on top of a hill with a wide view of mountains in the distance and plains below. But I found the place uninspiring, devoid of charm—mostly built or rebuilt in the nineteenth century, cold and too big.

Next it was Veszprém, another church town. It has a magnificent baroque archbishop's residence and an imposing cathedral that dates back to the time of Saint Stephen, about 1000. There's also a school run by Piarist monks, where András's father was a pupil. I'm not quite sure why he went to a Christian school, though András explained it. He's very concerned about his father these days. The old gentleman just spent two weeks in the hospital, and according to András he is getting weaker every day. He whines and complains like a child if András leaves him alone. "Poor man, now that he sees death near, he wants me there with him all the time." He's a good son, András.

Maybe the best part of the day was the end, when we

went for a swim in Lake Balaton before driving home. That's the advantage of a small country; you can cover a lot of ground before sunset. The water was clear and warm, wonderfully refreshing, and very few people were left on the beach by then.

András looks surprisingly good in a bathing suit. He wears the kind that slim men wear, close to the body, and his stomach hangs over it. His skin is smooth and firm; he looks better near naked than when he's dressed. That's because he dresses so badly. Today he was wearing an old grayish green T-shirt that was too small for him, pulling across the chest and belly. Every time I looked at him, I wished I could buy him a new one! It's not that he can't afford to buy one himself, he just doesn't seem to notice. I'm sure this is Mother's legacy again—she was always trying to "fix" people and was extremely judgmental about dress.

SUNDAY, JULY 11

A day to remember. I returned the car in the morning, and on the way I realized I could make a quick stop at the Collegium. I drove up there and got what I needed, then drove down again and found the tunnel that leads to the Chain Bridge, crossed the bridge, drove up József Attila Street, turned left on Bajcsy-Zsilinszky Avenue, and pulled into the rental place. Throughout, I had the exhilarating feeling of knowing my way, as if I were in Boston or Paris. After returning the car, I took the number 47 tram home. As we were crossing the Freedom Bridge, with the bright blue sky above and the shimmering river below, I suddenly thought, this could be the plot of my diary, the gradual move over the months here to a feeling of "at homeness." Until this year Budapest was not part of my life, not really. It *had been* in my life, but then I left it behind. Forgot it. When I returned in 1984 with the boys, that trip made me start writing about Budapest and my childhood. But my relation to the city remained that of a tourist. It's only now that I've lived here and made friends that I can think of Budapest as another home.

Mind you, it's not my "real home, found again at last." I'm too much of a foreigner for that, even if I do speak Hungarian. Yet it is one more home, indubitably. I feel happy here. The process of displacement/replacement, which I've thought of as the pattern of my life—each new home displacing the one before it—no longer holds: Budapest doesn't displace or replace any other home but is added to them. When I leave here, the door will not slam shut behind me.

The desire to find "my" Budapest, a Budapest I can call home, may be why I've resisted looking up the few distant family members I know remain here, even as I pursue my traces of the past. It's as if I had to make friends who can be part of my present life, of the person I am today, before venturing to make contact with those who represent only what once was. That's one reason András is so interesting to me, because he is both a link to the past—through his Jewishness, his intense sense of the Jews' suffering—and a link to the present, through his education, his profession, his interests.

This afternoon I went with him to see István Szabó's latest film, made in 1992. Szabó is known abroad as the director of *Mephisto* and *Meeting Venus*, but he has made many wonderful films in Hungarian—András has seen them all, and I've seen a couple as well. The new one, *Édes Emma, Drága Böbe* ("Dearest Emma, Darling Böbe"), is about two young provincial women who are schoolteachers in Budapest. They teach Russian in a high school and live on their meager salary in a teachers' dormitory. The first sign of "the Change" in 1989 is that they have to learn to teach English instead.

Budapest Diary

Szabó is merciless in showing the effects of "the Change" even on the smallest institutions: petty bickering among the teachers, desperate attempts by former Communists to divorce themselves from their Party past, and everywhere a generalized anxiety about the future. The story ends very badly: Böbe, the more defiant and apparently stronger of the two women, is arrested for prostitution, drug peddling, and illegal currency trafficking! In the meantime poor Emma is suffering because of an impossible love affair with her boss, the school principal, who suddenly becomes afraid for his reputation (he's married and has a family). Böbe is released from jail, comes to Emma's room for a shower and a change of clothes, then throws herself out the bathroom window. As for Emma, she apparently loses her job: the last shot in the film shows Emma in the subway station hawking newspapers, the way a much younger girl had done in an earlier scene. She screams the name of the paper: *Mai Nap, Mai Nap, Mai Nap, Mai Nap. Today, Today, Today, Today.* Bitter irony intended, of course: this is what today has come to.

Long discussion about the film with András afterward. There's a scene we talked about a lot where a crowd of women show up in a film studio to audition as extras. The director explains it's for a harem sequence in a historical film and they all have to be photographed naked; whoever doesn't want to do it should leave. But almost everyone stays, and Szabó shows them posing for their individual "mug shots," stark naked, each holding up a piece of paper with her name or number. As each one is photographed, she announces her profession: kindergarten teacher, elementary school teacher, waitress. All these women ready to humiliate themselves, allowing themselves to be treated like so many pieces of meat, are "good girls" with respectable professions; they simply can't make ends meet on their salaries. The naked mug shots remind one inevitably of the

172

way deportees were made to strip as the first step in their dehumanization. Those women being photographed frontally, their "numbers" above them, looked not very different from the Nazis' victims, totally vulnerable, totally exposed.

Szabó's position in all this is very complicated, because on the one hand he wants us to see these women as victims of the "new capitalism," but on the other hand he himself is implicated in the very thing he exposes. Elsewhere in the film he has several scenes of naked women in alluring poses—genuinely alluring, not victims like these women— so he too is in a sense exploiting his female actors, like the sleazy director in the film. The male actors are never shown naked, not even in a sex scene where the female star is undressed.

I told András I found the film too pessimistic—why did Böbe have to commit suicide? "Zsuzsa drága, darling Zsuzsa, you're a practical, rational American woman who can't even imagine how things are here. This is not pessimism, this is our reality!" Was this Hungarian melancholy speaking again? András tends to emphasize the negative in most things, I've noticed. But he sincerely meant it.

After the movie I went to the home of István and his wife, Ági, for dinner, just the three of us. They live beyond City Park in a six-story apartment building that looks like a typical piece of Stalinist architecture—ugly cinder blocks— but he told me it was built before the Stalinist period.

It turns out that not only is Ági Jewish, but her mother was at Auschwitz. The mother, who was nineteen in 1944, was deported with her parents, who were gassed immediately. Ági hasn't talked much to her mother about her war experiences. "Maybe if someone like you spoke to her, asked her questions, she'd remember things beyond the realm of the cliché," Ági said to me. But when I heard she'd been in Auschwitz, I suddenly felt afraid.

"It's too enormous. I'd feel too much responsibility stirring up those memories, then walking away," I told Ági. Maybe it's *because* I'd walk away that her mother could have talked to me. But I still can't imagine asking her, or anyone, "So tell me about Auschwitz."

I realized once again, this evening, how close to the horrors of history people are who live today in Budapest. Every Jewish adult living in this city has had at least one family member killed in the war. Some have lost their whole families and been deported themselves, like Ági's mother; others, like Farkas, were youngsters who escaped but lost a parent or other close relative to deportation or to the Nyilas. And yet people go about their business. They almost never talk about these things, and they don't go crazy, or not much. No wonder gallows humor thrives here. How else can one go on living after such devastation?

TUESDAY, JULY 13

After lunch I took the number 2 tram to the house of the filmmaker Pál Schiffer, whose film about the young gypsy impressed me so much when I saw it in April. Schiffer had offered to show me the videos of two of his other films; he greeted me cordially. He lives close to the Margit Bridge, in an apartment overlooking the Danube, with magnificent views of Parliament and the bridge and János Mountain across the river.

He put on the tape of *A Dunánál* ("By the Danube"), which is known in English as *Magyar Stories*. Schiffer explained that to a Hungarian audience the title evokes a well-known poem by the same title, which every schoolchild learns. He showed me the poem, by the great modernist poet Attila József; it's largely about what it means to be Hungarian. For József it meant being Slovak, Romanian, Turkish, and many other things as well—an "impure" view I find appealing. Schiffer popped in the video-cassette and made sure it was working, then wished me a pleasant time and left. The film is a detailed look at a village during the various Communist crackdowns after the war, as remembered by people many years later. I recognized Schiffer's style of narrative documentary, managing to render ordinary individuals as the dramatic heroes of their own lives.

He came back just as the video was ending and offered me coffee and fruit. Then he put on *Engesztelö*, which means "atonement." Made in 1989, after "the Change," this is a film about a woman and her two grown daughters, who try to uncover the truth of how and why her husband was killed by the secret police many years before. They get some answers, but not full disclosure, so both they and the viewer are left with a sense of frustration—and a sense of irreparable loss.

This time Schiffer stayed while I watched, and when the film ended we talked about how things were in Hungary after 1956. Right after the uprising, the Kádár regime was merciless, he said—and his films show that all too well. Then, about 1961, things began to change: the economy improved, everyone could afford to buy a car, maybe a country house, travel a bit. "At that point," Schiffer said, "Kádár and the Hungarian people made a deal. The people stayed out of politics, and the regime stayed out of their private lives. That pact worked for almost thirty years."

I'm taking the train early tomorrow morning for Nyíregyháza, Mother's birthplace.

WEDNESDAY, JULY 14

Up at 6:00 A.M., taxi to Nyugati station, where I caught the 7:20 express heading east. After Debrecen, I saw a brown-and-white cow lying on a grassy path next to the railroad tracks as we sped by. Otherwise the view struck me as totally indifferent, except for the large fields of sunflowers, growing tall and beautiful.

I don't know why I always imagined Nyíregyháza as a sleepy little village where kids ran around barefoot. It must have been because of Mother's story about the watermelons. When she and her sister Magdi and their brother Lester (then known as Laci) were kids, they often spent the summer holidays there, at an uncle's house; one day when the adults were gone, the kids and all their local friends, under Magdi's direction, cut up every watermelon in the house (the uncle had just had a truckload delivered), scraped out the red fruit, and used the green rinds as helmets! Mother used to tell this story with great relish, to illustrate their mischievousness and Magdi's ability to command or charm her peers. That's why I thought of Nyíregyháza as a village, a *falu*. In fact it's a large city, capital of three northeastern counties, with a proud city hall in the classical style overlooking a leafy square, several major churches, and many imposing buildings commissioned by banks or similar institutions around the turn of the century. I took lots of photos and walked almost everywhere and now feel exhausted. It was worth it.

At the train station I bought a detailed map and walked to the city hall—down Petöfi Avenue, turn right on Széchenyi Avenue, past the museum and several banks, through a pedestrian mall, and finally to Kossuth Lajos Square—the same heroes everywhere. I went into the city hall looking for the Motherbook Office. Unbelievable. I was directed to another building on the mall, where a pleasant-looking woman asked me what I wanted. I explained, gave Mother's name and birth date (the real one), and went off to buy the required 300 forints of stamps at the post office around the corner. By the time I came back a few minutes later, she had found everything and typed up the document. "Excerpt from the Motherbook: Birth certificate for Lili Stern, girl, born on July 27, 1908, in Nyíregyháza. Father's name: Mózes Stern; mother's name: Rézi Lebovics."

"Her name was Lili, not Livia as you told me," said Mrs. Tibor Csapó, who had signed the document. She sounded almost reproachful.

"I'm sorry, I thought her official name was Livia even though everyone called her Lili. See, that's what it says on her marriage certificate." I pulled out the envelope with the certificate from my bag, for I had brought it along as András had suggested.

"Yes, it is Livia there," Mrs. Csapó conceded. Curious, this alternation of names for no apparent reason. Is Livia more grand, or less Jewish, than Lili?

I noticed the birth certificate didn't list a home address. "Is it possible to know where she was born?" I asked Mrs. Csapó.

"Well, in Nyíregyháza," she answered.

"No, I mean the address—where she lived." She went out and came back a few minutes later.

"Pazsonyi Ut 7."

"Does that road still exist?"

"Yes, it does." I took out the map and after a bit of looking she found it. "It's out next to the Northern Cemetery." On the map it said "Pazsonyi utca," street, not "ut," avenue or road.

It didn't seem too far, so I decided to walk there. As I was looking at the map again, my eye fell on the words *Izraelita temetö*, Jewish cemetery, some distance from Pazsonyi Street. I decided to go there too, later.

Pazsonyi Street is dusty. It runs literally along the Northern Cemetery, with houses on only one side. Actually they're not real houses, but what look like workshops or storage sheds; some buildings stand in small lots strewn with stones: tombstone carvers. Number 7, clearly marked (Pazsonyi utca 7, blue plaque) has a metal fence, and behind it a small low building and stones. Obviously this was not the house where Mother was born. I asked a woman sitting in a car in front whether Pazsonyi Street was the same as Pazsonyi Road. She said Pazsonyi Road was off to the right, where a car was turning. I walked that way, but it was marked Hunyadi Road. I walked back and saw her again on the corner.

"No luck?" she asked.

"No, it was Hunyadi Road."

"Yes, but it's actually the road to Pazsony, so it's the Pazsonyi Road even though it has a different name." Yet another name game—but by then I was too tired to walk back again and see whether number 7 was a plausible house, so I took a couple of photos on Pazsonyi Street and asked the woman to take one of me in front of the metal gate with the number 7 plaque behind me.

"Probably they tore down the original house," she said, after I explained what I was looking for.

"Yes, it was long ago."

I said good-bye and headed for the Jewish cemetery. I took a bus for three stops but still had a long walk in the sun. Suddenly, on a fenced hillside to my right, I saw the tombstones. I found a gate and a walk leading to a small house. A man came out, and I asked whether I could go into the cemetery.

"Of course, come right in." He and his wife were the caretakers. Who was I looking for?

"I'm not sure, but two names are Lebovits and Stern."

"We have those," he said. He took me up the hill to a large stone archway covered all over with carved names— hundreds of them, thousands. This was the memorial to the deported and killed: 17,000 Jews from Nyíregyháza died in the camps, the short text said. We couldn't find any Sterns or Lebovitses among the names, but "leave us your address and we'll look for them," the caretaker said. I left him behind and walked on among the gravestones. There were many, some very imposing in black marble or large carved stones, others more modest: Szamuely, Hegedüs, Havas, Moskovits, all the names looked familiar. The tombs covered a wooded green hillside, very calm and clean and peaceful. I took photos, then walked back toward the memorial and was met by the caretaker and his wife. "She found the Lebovits family," he called out. On the bottom of the memorial and to the side was the inscription "Lebovits család"—they were not listed individually, just once as a family. It was my maternal grandmother's maiden name. We also found some Sterns, three of them.

Too tired. I'll continue tomorrow.

FRIDAY, JULY 16

The caretaker and his wife were very helpful: "Just let us know who you're looking for, and we'll try to find them," the husband said. I thought possibly he might find tombstones of people who had died natural deaths before 1944. I gave him 500 forints as I left.

The caretakers told me there's a functioning synagogue in Nyíregyháza and even a Jewish Community Bureau. (András was incredulous when I told him this. "Aw, go on." Yes, there are about one hundred Jewish families living in the county, if not in Nyíregyháza proper.) I took a taxi to the address they had given me, closer to the center of town. The synagogue, on a corner next to some trees, is not impressive from the outside. It looks squeezed into its space, unlike the imposing synagogues in Pécs and Györ. A semitoothless man who looked like the concierge let me into the courtyard and took me up a few steps to the office.

The woman who received me was small, elderly, with dark olive skin, white hair, a pained and anxious look on her face. "She looks Jewish," I said to myself. She introduced herself in the traditional style ("Mrs. Husband's Name," including his first name, obliterating her name completely) and said she was the Bureau's secretary. Then a tall, upright old man came in, wearing a yarmulke—the president of the congregation. The three of us sat at the long table and talked. His name, I soon found out, is Ignácz P. What a nice, sturdy name Ignácz is.

Ignácz P. used to work for a local factory but is now retired and owns a farm. "I was a kulak in the old days," he said with a laugh. He speaks with a provincial accent and has a large, rugged face that could be that of any village dignitary. We talked for a while about the current situation in Hungary.

"Horrible," he said. "Those politicians are eating everything up [he used the word that refers to sheep or cows grazing]; in the end there'll be nothing left." His colleague agreed: "In forty years Kádár didn't manage to persuade us about the evils of capitalism. Over the past three years, we finally learned!" Before leaving I gave a donation to the synagogue; she filled out a receipt in duplicate and gave me a copy.

Ignácz P. took me to look at the inside of the synagogue—newly redecorated, with pastel decorations painted on the white walls. He is very proud of the place. "Thanks to the support of Jews from abroad, we were able to do it," he said. He's also proud about how well kept the cemetery is. "Good, isn't it?" he asked. Yes. Every year on the Yom Hashoah, the anniversary of the Holocaust, they have a memorial service at the martyrs' monument.

Not too many Jews in Nyíregyháza today. And those that remain are not very interested in religion. "I often talk about it with my wife, whether I should step down as pres-

Enormous Changes

ident," Ignácz P. said. "But if I didn't do it, there would be no one else." He stood there in the afternoon sun, smiling, white haired, his large yarmulke almost covering his head—a big, provincial Jewish man I wanted very much to photograph. But I didn't. I simply shook his hand and said good-bye.

At the train station I saw a fruit stand with a small pile of watermelons on the ground. In honor of Mother's mischievous childhood, I photographed the round, dark green, very helmetlike melons.

SATURDAY, JULY 17

It's past midnight, technically July 18, and I am fifty-four years old. I gave a Midsummer Night's party tonight, which was also, sad to say, a farewell party. No one knew it was a birthday party as well except András, who arrived bearing gifts of records and books. Thanks to him, I now have a respectable library of modern Hungarian poetry; tonight he brought the complete works of Miklós Radnóti, a Jewish poet killed by the Nazis, who left his greatest poems in a small rain-soaked notebook that was found buried near his body after his death. András also brought a two-volume set of prose works by the writers of *Nyugat*, the influential review founded just before World War I. Such a dear man, András. I discovered a whole new side of him tonight: he's an excellent dancer, extremely agile despite his girth, and loves to dance. We did the jitterbug, sixties style.

The rector brought an enormous bunch of sunflowers and a copy of Krudy's *Szindbád*, beautifully wrapped. He gave it to me with a laugh, even more boisterous than usual, since I had told him I didn't like the movie. "Now you'll see whether you like the book," he joked. Others brought more flowers—the house looks like a bower. The

181

sunflowers are stupendous; I've never seen them in bouquets, only in the fields.

Eva came with her tall engineer husband, whom I've met a few times. Farkas and his wife were here, along with a bunch of others from the Collegium, including Robert, Stani, and Sanda. Tibor and Anna have already returned to Paris. Aniko came without Peter; he had to stay home to baby-sit. Ilona and Gábor were here too—I hadn't seen them for a while. I'm scheduled to go on a "Budapest walk" with Gábor later this week. Dezsö also came, the sociologist who attended my Collegium lecture. He's an unusually attractive young man and has a way of looking at you that makes your heart melt, very soulful. He got along splendidly with Gábor and Ilona, and with András. They were the last four to leave.

"Has Budapest become one of the places you can call home?" asked Dezsö. Actually, he stated it rather than asking—and added: "I envy you. Some of us don't have homes anywhere, and you have three homes."

He was being coy, I pointed out to him. "I saw your family's name in a book of photographs about Nyíregyháza. It was attached to a castle."

"That was long ago," he said.

"Well, I wouldn't count you among the homeless." He comes from an old noble family, András told me. But he claims his was the "poor, minor" branch.

My last birthday party in this country was forty-four years ago. Mother had a table set up in the garden of the summer house, and we invited all my friends from the pool club. We ate cake and fruit and ice cream; Mother unveiled my birthday present from her and Daddy, a shiny new red-and-chrome bicycle. It was perfect, just what I had longed for. I was so happy I dreamed about it for several nights afterward. The bicycle was one of the things I most regretted leaving behind when we left home a few weeks later.

Enormous Changes

How do I feel, being fifty-four? The same as I did yesterday, when I was fifty-three. But I may be fooling myself, pretending the accumulation of years doesn't matter. Let's not dwell on that.

SUNDAY, JULY 18

A very sightseeing kind of afternoon, spent with András. We went up to the historical museum in the Castle, where excavators found medieval remains when they rebuilt it after the war. There's a whole roomful of beautiful statues from the late fourteenth century, the reign of King Zsigmond—some very typical Hungarian heads, in particular a mustachioed man wearing a kind of Oriental headdress. Also some traditional angels, with rich drapery. András pointed out from the window the pieces of castle wall that had been completely buried until the postwar excavations. The castle was badly bombed during the fighting, and it took decades to get it back into shape. Maybe that's why I had no memory of it or of that whole neighborhood. It's possible I never even went up there after the war.

Our plan was to walk down through the "new" gardens from the castle to the Elizabeth Bridge and then up to the top of Mount Gellért. András hurried me along, and in the end I was glad he did, because the view from the sloping gardens is truly splendid. One in particular, with the Tabán Church in the foreground and the bridge in the background, caught my fancy. "I show this only to people I'm very fond of," András said.

When we got to the bottom, we tried to find a taxi to take us to the top of Mount Gellért, but since we had no luck I suggested we walk. "What? It'll take an hour!" András protested. But in fact it took us only thirty minutes, even with a stop halfway up to look at the statue of Saint Gellért about to be hurled to his martyrdom by a pagan.

The second half of the climb was somewhat strenuous, but not too bad. The view from the top was superb, just as András had promised. He showed me the empty space on the monument where the colossal Soviet soldier had once stood. That statue was one of the first to be taken down after "the Change."

András fished from his pocket a small piece of paper he had saved for me. It was the wrapping from a piece of processed cheese, featuring a photo of the monument with the soldier still on it! Apparently they forgot to change the logo after 1989. "A small overlooked detail that speaks volumes about our recent history," he commented.

I found two messages from Judy and one from Danny when I got home, wishing me a happy birthday. No message from Michael yet, but it's still early evening on the East Coast; already July 19 for me, the day after my birthday.

I haven't mentioned our Collegium trip to Eger on Friday. This time only a few people went. Lovely city, Eger, another bishopric full of ecclesiastical buildings. It also has a fortress from which the women poured boiling oil on the attacking Turks in the sixteenth century. The Turks finally conquered the town, and one can still see a minaret among the church towers.

We passed in front of a building that was once part of the synagogue, now carrying the sign of a furniture store—but even the store has moved to new quarters, so the building is closed. "They blew up the synagogue," András said bitterly when I told him about the trip this afternoon. "Vicious Nazi town, Eger. It's the headquarters of our native skinheads, a lot of whom are the sons of good bourgeois families." That's not the kind of information tour guides like to give out, and ours was no exception.

In the grand basilica, which we visited at noon for an organ recital, I noticed a statue surrounded by small stone tablets. When I went closer, I saw they were ex-votos bearing inscriptions of thanks. ("Thanks for the help; keep it up.") A plaque above the statue informed the visitor that this was a shrine of Saint Rita, the patroness of those in "apparently hopeless situations." Her specialty is bringing help at the last minute, when all seems lost; for that reason I will call her, in honor of Grace Paley's wonderful stories, the patroness of Enormous Changes at the Last Minute. She must be a cousin of the "Virgen de los desemparados," the "Virgin of the Lost Ones," whose church I saw a few weeks ago in Valencia.

Do I feel like a *desemparada*? No, I can't say that. But I think I'm always hoping for enormous changes at the last minute.

MONDAY, JULY 19

Meeting with Tamás Raj, brother of our rabbi in Belmont, Massachusetts. He's a rabbi too, but in 1990 he was elected to Parliament. We met at the "White House," once the Party headquarters where Kádár throned, now the office building for members of Parliament. At the entrance, a soldier was asking guests to state their business. I gave Raj's name, but he hadn't arrived yet. Just as the soldier was calling his office he walked in—a slightly stooped, bearded, kind-faced man who looks more like a rabbi than an MP. He wears a rabbinical hat that lets two sidelocks (*payes*) show; they're cut very short, so it's not clear they're really sidelocks, but with the hat they immediately gave me that impression.

We went to the buffet on the ground floor behind the large hall, but it was closed, so we got coffee from a machine and sat in armchairs in the main hall. I asked him how he forecasts next year's election. "The Communists will

win," he said. (He meant the ex-Communists, now called
Socialists.)

"Really?

"Sure. The MDF has made such a mess of things, people
are sorry the old times are gone."

"But you're not sorry?"

"No." He was arrested a couple of times in the late 1960s
and early 1970s because he insisted on teaching Talmud
to university students. He smiled: "What's a rabbi who
doesn't teach?"

"Then what are you doing in politics?" I asked.

"I'm not a politician; in fact I'm not going to run again.
But it was important to show that if there was a Jew in a
yarmulke in the Communist Parliament, there had to be
one in this Parliament too."

Who were the previous religious Jews? A rabbi named
Salgó, and then another one named Schöner. "Do you re-
act each time you hear an anti-Semitic remark?" I asked. He
shook his head: "I'm not a politician, but I do know a good
politician is not completely predictable. If I reacted every
time, they could always foresee what I was going to say.
It's important not to do that. They should never know
when I'm going to say something, or what I'm going to
say when I do."

"What do you think of Hungarian Jews? Are most of
them still somewhat ashamed to say they're Jewish?"

"Well, it's certainly not like America. People are often
afraid to say they're Jewish. But the main thing is *not* to be
afraid, because people can always tell and they'll hound
you. Anyway, even if you try to hide that you're a Jew, the
others always know."

He smiled. "Here, I'll tell you a story. About twenty
years ago, when I was just starting out as a rabbi, I had to
go from my synagogue in Szeged to a small town on some
business. The president of the Community Bureau was

supposed to meet my train, but at the last minute he fell ill and couldn't come. Nobody was waiting for me at the station, and I had no idea where I was supposed to go. So I started walking, and after a while I stopped somebody on the street and told him I was a rabbi. Could he tell me where the Jewish Community Bureau was? No, he really didn't know. Well, what about the Jewish neighborhood? Where did the Jews in town live? 'There's a Jew living in that house over there,' the man answered and pointed to a house nearby. I started walking toward the house, but the man ran after me. 'On second thought, rabbi, you'd better not go to him. You see, only we know he's Jewish. He doesn't know it.'"

A stunning story. There was nothing to add.

He asked if there was something special he could do for me, but all I could think of was to mention the hunt for Daddy's traces at the Orthodox Community Bureau and my thought that the records may have been transferred to the Reform Bureau on Sip Street. "Maybe," he said. He himself had gone to the Kazinczy Street synagogue as a child. "I'm two and a half years older than my brother," he said. "Born in February 1940." That means he's younger than I am by a few months. Once more, confirmation that men age quickly in these parts. Almost every one of the Hungarians I've met here looks older than his age.

He had another appointment, but before I left he took me over to look behind the curtain that covers the large wall we had been sitting near. In front of the curtain hangs an oversize Hungarian shield, with the crown of Saint Stephen on top.

"You see, that's what this government cared about—to revive the crown as on the prewar shield. They were more interested in ideology than in the economy; that was their mistake," he said.

Behind the curtain is a fresco painted under the Kádár regime, at the same time the building was constructed. He described it to me before showing it: "Down below, the workers busily toiling; above them, the Party leaders sitting around and talking, smoking cigarettes." What we saw when we lifted the curtain was a little less blatantly hierarchical than that, because the people on top are dressed exactly the same as the workers below: T-shirt and pants, as if to suggest the two groups are interchangeable. Still, there's a clearly marked separation between above and below, so in that Raj was right.

After our meeting I walked the few steps to Margit Bridge and got on a tram heading for the Oktogon. András told me yesterday that the Oktogon, right in the middle of Andrássy Avenue, was called Hitler Square during the 1930s!

I'm seriously contemplating a last-minute trip to Poland. It turns out that Daddy's birthplace, Gorlice, is not far from Cracow, and to go to Cracow takes only about six hours by car. There are no easy train or bus connections, and Stani has discouraged me from driving over the Tatra Mountains, but the filmmaker Márta Mészáros (whom I met in Cambridge a few years ago) told me on the phone tonight that it's an easy trip. She's done it many times; her husband is from Cracow. Stani will call Gorlice's city hall for me tomorrow, to speak to them in Polish. If they have Daddy's birth certificate, I'll go. I'd like to find someone to go with me. András can't leave his father alone overnight.

Tomorrow I'm taking Mother's cousin Cica out to dinner. I last saw her in Paris in 1984, and I haven't called her since I've been here. Everything in its own time.

TUESDAY, JULY 20

To my amazement, this afternoon Gábor offered to accompany me to Poland. It was during our Budapest walk, when he showed me his favorite spots. You could have knocked me over with a feather. "But do you really have time for this trip?" I asked. (I was dying to add, but didn't: "And what will Ilona say?")

"I love to travel," he replied simply. In principle, we will leave early Friday morning, in time to arrive in Gorlice while the city hall is still open. After that, we'll go on to visit Cracow and return on Saturday. But I won't really believe it until it happens. It's too unexpected, too crazy.

Whatever else one can say about him, Gábor is an adventurous man; a very attractive one too. And what about my great high-horse principle about not starting anything with married men? Well, I never intended or expected this. Besides, nothing has happened, and perhaps nothing will. In the meantime we are to meet for a quick dinner on Thursday night before starting our dawn trip to Poland.

We went to look at a new building Gábor likes, not too far from Acacia Street. It's actually an old building to which a new top half has been added, very postmodern; although totally unlike, the two halves go together strikingly well. It was designed by the architect Imre Makovecz, who has won a lot of prizes. Makovecz has some hateful ideas about "true Hungarianness," Gábor said.

"You mean he's a Csurka fan?"

"Well, probably not that far—but he's the darling of the MDF. Let's go look at the new entrance to the zoo, OK?"

I don't know why, but that quick transition made me burst out laughing. There's something very playful about Gábor, which I like a lot.

I did my duty by the *parenthèse* today, as Proust's character Françoise would say: Sándor in the morning, and his divorced wife Cica at dinner. They were both very glad to see me. Sándor described at great length the day my aunt Magdi died while visiting Budapest and how he had to break the news to her brother Lester; he talked almost exclusively about the old friends he has buried over the past few years. Cica was a bit more cheerful (she's a very well preserved woman in her seventies, with dyed blond hair and silk scarves), but she too has stories about illness, old age, and death. Both of her parents were killed at Auschwitz. She and her sister escaped deportation because they were in Budapest, and the deportations stopped in time to spare the capital (here it was only the Arrow Cross men who murdered Jews).

Cica told me a naughty story about Daddy: "He liked beautiful women. In fact, there was a great scandal the day your mother discovered him with a woman in the maid's room on Acacia Street—he had taken her there because they didn't have a maid at the time." Well! I knew about the beautiful lady in Vienna, but I didn't know about any women in Budapest. I guess he really wasn't cut out to be a rabbi.

Of course Cica may have the story all wrong—her memory is notoriously faulty, as she told me when it came time to talk about the Stern family (we put that off until our next meeting). The only thing I find truly shocking in the story she told (if it's true) is that he'd take a woman to his own house. That shows a lack of tact so great it offends me and makes him look extremely low. Can I imagine how Mother felt? Yes, I can.

The more I write this diary, the closer I feel to Mother. For better or worse.

WEDNESDAY, JULY 21

Phone rang this morning, it was Gábor. I was sure he was calling to say he had changed his mind, especially after the first words, which were apologetic. But he only proposed putting off the trip, because Friday-Saturday was not good. So we agreed on Sunday-Monday, reversing the order: Cracow first, Gorlice on the way back. Before I hung up, I was seized with scruples: "Just one thing—people sometimes say things they'd like to do, and later for some reason it doesn't work out. Please don't feel obliged or tied down by what you said yesterday. If you can't make it after all, I'll understand."

"Oh, no, now it's decided; we're going on Sunday-Monday and that's it," he answered. I'll reserve the car tomorrow, but I still don't completely believe this trip will take place. If only he weren't married!

Failed to get a copy of my city hall birth certificate today— it was not in the eighth district, as I had thought. The woman in the eighth district's Motherbook Office claimed there were never any deliveries at the Bókay Street children's hospital. So why was that the address given in the registry at the Community Bureau? No idea. Next I tried the seventh district, where I knew they must have the marriage certificate if nothing else. They did, but that's all they had. Now I possess a second copy of this document, much less picturesque and poorer in information than the 1947 version. No addresses given, no mention of profession, and of course no indication of religion. Mother's birth date is the correct one, 1908, as I knew it would be.

Where was I born, if not in the eighth district and not in the seventh?

THURSDAY, JULY 22

Nasty, rainy day today. It poured without interruption until about 6:00 P.M., and this was the day I had reserved with András to go to the Orthodox cemetery!

Budapest Diary

The afternoon began early, with a visit to András and his father; this involved buying pastries at Café Gerbeaud and flowers on Váci Street, and also the present of a crystal vase for András that I've been planning to get for a while. All in the pouring rain. By the time I arrived at their apartment, about 1:00, my shoes were thoroughly soaked and so were the sleeves of my raincoat and blouse.

András's father is a frail-looking, dignified man who said to me while András was in the kitchen, "I only wish it would all end soon." He was on the verge of tears, and in that moment of self-pity and frustration he reminded me very much of Mother in her last year. I suspect that, like her, he doesn't really mean it when he says he wishes his life would end. I think it's just the opposite; he's afraid it will end all too soon.

He bosses András around, as Mother used to do with me. "Get a plate," when I showed him the pastries. "Wash out the glass," when he gave me, as a return gift for the vase, a champagne goblet he took out of a glass cabinet. András does his bidding, even if with some impatience: "Wait a minute, Daddy dear." Before we left, I asked whether he thought his father would like me to photograph him. "Oh, yes, it would give him much pleasure." So I took a couple of pictures of the old gentleman, sitting upright in his chair and looking solemn. I also took one of father and son together.

After the visit, as we were going downstairs, András told me, "My father is madly in love with you."

"How can you tell?" I asked.

"After forty-five years of living with him, I can tell." He is a good son.

The trip to the cemetery was a total failure. I hadn't called ahead, thinking the guard would be there. But he wasn't—someone told us he had left a few minutes before we arrived. Since the Orthodox cemetery doesn't have any clear markings to indicate the placing of the graves, it did me no good to have written down the locations Mr. H. had given me; the rows, as far as we could see, were unmarked, and after wandering around for a while among the gravestones in the pouring rain, we had to give up. All the writing on the stones is in Hebrew, so we couldn't use that as much help either. I was able to read some of the names, but none corresponded to those I was looking for.

In short, a wasted trip. By then my shoes were drenched through and through and my feet were frigid. We got back in the taxi. The cemetery is far out, almost an hour's drive, and it's unlikely I'll have time to visit it again before I leave. The grave I'm most sorry to have missed is that of my little brother, András Rubin.

This outing was so badly botched that I wonder whether it wasn't an *acte manqué*, a willed failure. Considering how far the cemetery is and how little time remains, and that I had the guard's phone number, it's astounding I didn't call ahead. Even in 1984 I had no desire to find out anything about the cemetery, though my aunt Rózsi had visited it more than once. And when Judy came to Hungary on a short trip a few years ago, she made a point of visiting our grandparents' graves with Sam and the children. In the end, I think I have a deep dislike of cemeteries. Did I really need this botched job to find that out?

Dinner with Gábor, in a restaurant created out of an old basement. We were there from 8:00 until past 11:00, talking and planning our trip. He's very into it now—he even drew up an itinerary on his computer and gave me a copy. We're meeting on Saturday morning at the car rental place to sign up for driving the car. It looks as if this trip will take place.

When he drove me home and stopped at the curb, he kept looking up at the apartment, but I didn't invite him up. We sat for a few minutes in the car, then kissed on the cheeks, and I thanked him for the lovely evening. "It was a very wonderful evening," he said before he drove away.

A day jammed with activity as I try to cross things off my list. About noon I went to the Reform Community Bureau on Sip Street to inquire about Daddy and was received kindly but with a firm no. Very few records of any kind remain, and certainly none regarding employees of the Orthodox Bureau before the war. So I struck out again. I suppose I could try harder, seek different channels—but to tell the truth, the search for concrete traces is beginning to wear me down. The trip to Poland will be my last try.

Stani has been a great help in trying to get in touch with Gorlice, but today we had no luck. By the time the operators got through, no one was picking up the phone at the city hall. There's no time to try again before the trip, so we'll have to wing it. Stani wrote a letter in Polish, addressed to the woman he spoke to on Wednesday, asking her to help me.

Afternoon with Tamás F., photographing in the old neighborhood. I want a picture taken in Budapest for the dust jacket of *Risking Who One Is*. Tamás, a rather well known photographer, was recommended by someone at the Collegium. He shot two rolls of black-and-white photos—on Dob Street, near the Kazinczy Street synagogue, next to the big synagogue on Dohány Street, in the courtyard of 59 Acacia Street, and in the old indoor market that is now owned by a supermarket chain.

Afterward, at the Müvész Café, we talked. He's only a year older than I am, and he lived a couple of blocks away as a child. "We probably passed each other on the street on the way to school, about 1948," he said. He spent the last year of the war in the ghetto, in this very neighborhood, and he remembers fishing for boxes of crackers that had gotten mixed in among a pile of dead bodies behind a railing on Klauzal Square. "You know, it was the horror, but we kids didn't see it that way. We even had fun. We played. You must admit, it's the tops when you end up fishing for crackers among corpses."

Hungarian gallows humor. One thing I find incongruous (but perhaps it's less so than I think) is that he's a hunter. A real hunter, who goes out with a gun and shoots animals. Last week he shot a wild boar, and it wasn't even for eating, just for the sport. He could pass for a Hungarian peasant: his body is small, stocky, thick like a countryman's, and he wears flannel shirts. But his eyes give him away, for they are deep and soft and sad.

Movie this evening with András, and afterward we went to a renovated pub near the movie house for a bite to eat. I couldn't help thinking of last night's dinner with Gábor. András strikes me as not very comfortable with intimacy. He protects himself from it by becoming the guide and storyteller—he often talks rapidly and for a long time without making eye contact. What he says is often deep and always well informed, but because of that strangely impersonal quality it lacks the excitement and interest of a conversation with Gábor. I feel almost guilty writing this. András is a devoted friend, and it feels like a betrayal to analyze him as if he were a character in a novel.

Last night, as we left the restaurant, Gábor suddenly said, "Everything is coming together for you now, isn't it?" I was surprised by how attuned he was to my mood. I told him about Grace Paley and *Enormous Changes at the Last Minute*, and about Saint Rita. Something new is happening to me during these last days in Budapest.

Budapest Diary

Left Budapest at 7:10 A.M., arrived here at 1:30 after a fif-teen-minute stop at the Slovak frontier, where they took most of our forints—to be returned on the way back. Also made a couple of photo stops, plus a fruitless attempt at coffee in Slovakia: Gábor had koronas, but they couldn't change his large bill. Gorgeous castle in a village just before Z(?).

We told stories in the car, Gábor driving all the way. His father was a professor of anthropology at Debrecen, from a family of Protestant ministers.

Cracow busy with milling Sunday crowds.

To be continued.

TUESDAY, JULY 27

My last full day in Budapest. Running, running. Farewell dinner at the Collegium this evening, before I rushed home to finish packing. The rector was there, as well as Trevor and his girlfriend (to close the circle—it seems an eternity since he picked me up at the airport), Robert, Stani, and others. I took photos, as usual. Great good cheer all around, though I doubt that some of us will see each other again.

I feel fonder than ever of Stani, after his help and in-volvement with the Gorlice trip. He came rushing up to me, breathless for news of how it went. I gave him a brief but effusive account, and he seemed very pleased. He was sorry I didn't have Pan Boczon's books with me, he would have liked to see them and translate for me; but I told him I can get Polish friends in Cambridge to help me out. The written account of the trip will have to wait until I'm back home. It would take far too long to tell in detail now, and that's how I want to tell it.

Enormous Changes

This morning, the journalist I met at Márta's house on Saturday came over for our interview. She works for a women's magazine, covering the cultural beat. She asked me about women in America, how I came to be doing what I do, what I think of Hungarian academics, pretty much the usual stuff. But the most interesting moment came at the end, when she shut off the tape recorder and asked, off the record, Did I think Hungarian women looked older than their age, and did I have anxieties about age?

"You see, I'm just forty, and for the first time I'm finding myself worrying about looking older. You're an attractive woman, so I was just wondering . . ." and her voice trailed off. Fascinating! During the interview I had been aware I wasn't hiding my age, since I spoke about my childhood and how old I was when I left Budapest. It was a conscious, not totally easy choice. Now, suddenly, she revealed her own anxieties about aging, but only with the tape recorder turned off. There seemed to be almost a reversal of roles, as if the interviewer had become the subject of the interview.

In fact, I would have thought she was older than forty. She has bleached blond hair, and her face is set into firm lines—two long ones run down the sides of her cheeks, giving her a somewhat harsh, dissatisfied look. Her self-revelation made her seem more vulnerable, softer. I asked whether she found life after Communism disappointing. No, she said, but it's hard. "I tell myself we've got another twenty years before things will be better. That means my whole generation is a sacrificed generation. Things will be better for my daughter, but for me it'll be too late." After that I understood a little better why she has those two deep lines on her face.

The interview should appear in the fashion magazine about October. There will even be a photo of me, one of the ones taken by Tamás. Mother would have been proud.

Lunch with Cica and her sister Marika at Café Gerbeaud. Marika is the very opposite of Cica, a bitter woman who likes to tell people the most disagreeable things about themselves "for their own good" or "for the sake of the truth." To me, for example, she announced gleefully that she had heard from my uncle Nick about the young man I was in love with in college, whose family "broke the engagement when they heard your father wasn't really a rabbi." There was no point in trying to correct her, so I didn't try. We had already had an altercation earlier when we spoke about Lester and Izsó, Mother's two brothers. "I wasn't speaking to Lester for the past twenty years—he didn't behave well with us when we visited Miami Beach," she said. "But Izsó was a fine man, died in forced labor."

"Yes, and Lester too was in forced labor, but he came back," I said.

"I don't know anything about that," came the reply.

"Well, I'm telling you he was in forced labor," I said sharply. I had to repeat it twice, getting angrier each time. Evidently, since she wasn't on speaking terms with Lester in the later part of his life, she didn't want to admit anything positive about him even from an earlier time. Not that being in forced labor was something positive—but it put him in the role of victim, and she wants to think of herself as the victim of his bad treatment. Cica, who was also on that visit to Miami Beach twenty years ago, continued to see Lester right up to his death. Some people are able to forgive, others not. Mystery.

On the other hand (there's always that other hand), Marika has plenty to be bitter about. Both her parents died at Auschwitz. Her brother Zoltán, a doctor, was made to dig his own grave and then was shot into it by the Nazis on his thirty-fifth birthday, in the spring of 1945. Like the poet Radnóti, whose collected verse András gave me for my birthday.

Enormous Changes

On the third hand, Cica had exactly the same parents and the same brother. Perhaps the difference is that Marika has a better memory. Thus it was she who was able to give me a complete account of the Stern family in its various branches. Cica, by her own admission, has very little knowledge of precise facts, and her sense of time is extremely skewed—she can't remember what year things occurred, whereas Marika has a sharp awareness of dates and places. Of course she cruelly puts Cica down whenever she makes a mistake.

Here, then, is what she told me about the Stern family, Mother's paternal aunts and uncles: there were eight siblings in all, including Mother's father—a large family, and Moses was the only one who settled in Budapest. His brothers Simon and Samu Stern lived in Nyíregyháza with their families; they were the ones Grandmother must have been visiting when Mother was born, and she continued to visit them while the children were young. Simon was a shopkeeper with five children, and Samu was a bit of a schlemiel; he had two daughters and a son named István (there was an István Stern inscribed on the memorial monument in the cemetery).

Cica's and Marika's father, whose name was David Stern, lived in Losoncz, a small town that's now in Czechoslovakia, as did another brother Izsó (not to be confused with Mother's brother, my uncle Izsó). Izsó's wife was the Zsazsa Néni I visited with Michael and Daniel on our trip in 1984—she had been living in Budapest for many years, childless, and had never remarried. Her husband was killed in the war, along with all the other family members who lived in Losoncz. Besides the four brothers (five counting my grandfather), there were three sisters—two lived in Losoncz and one in Ungvár, Grandmother's and Grandfather's birthplace, now Uzhgorod in Ukraine.

As far as my grandfather Moses Stern is concerned, Cica

remembers visiting him in the hospital shortly before he died—she must have been a little girl at the time. Marika, who's younger, doesn't remember him at all. It seems certain that he didn't die as a result of a "beating by a Hungary Firster," as Milton thought. But he did die very young, and his death spelled decline for the family. Mother was not quite sixteen when she lost her father. Another parallel between us: I had just turned twenty when Daddy died.

Today is Mother's birthday. She would have been eighty-five years old. I had thought of leaving Budapest today, for the poetic closure of it, but it would have been too complicated, since there are no nonstop flights to New York on Tuesdays. And if I had booked the return flight for today, I couldn't have gone to Cracow and Gorlice. So it all turned out for the best, even in the absence of poetry.

＊

WEDNESDAY, JULY 28—*Plane over the Atlantic*

In this state of suspension above water, my head is full of images. Gábor's hands on the steering wheel, extraordinarily big and capable looking: I keep staring at them as we talk. The arrival in Cracow, finding a parking place in the city center so we can go exploring. Gábor turns to me, playful, parodying the "good wife": "Darling, you decide what we should do. Where should we go first?"

Rarely have I played with a man like that.

The central market square, Rynek Glowny, was milling with pigeons and Sunday crowds. Children played as the birds flew around them, the café terraces were full, and the sun shone brightly on the double towers of the great brick Church of Our Lady and the other old edifices on the square. We walked around, took photographs, sat in a famous, dark art nouveau café, then found a hotel near the old city walls. We took separate rooms. At dinnertime we went out again and found the Grand Hotel, where they served us shashlik on a flaming sword. In one part of the room a wedding party was feasting and dancing.

When we left the restaurant it was raining—a gentle rain, easy to walk in. Near our hotel we saw a disco club and went in: loud music, low lights; we were the oldest dancers in the room. We stayed there until 2:00A.M., dancing almost nonstop. Then a short walk along the glistening, deserted street (the rain had stopped) and five hours of sleep before the challenging day.

He had asked me earlier what I thought would be the best hotel arrangement. I replied, hypocritically, "I don't know." In a way it was true, I didn't know, or at least didn't want to be responsible for the decision. He didn't want to be responsible for it either, and I think I understand why. As long as things are light and playful, he is willing to transgress—but his life is not set up for heavy sentimental transactions. He must have sensed a huge layer of heavy sentiment beneath my banter and decided—wisely—to back off.

Why can't I be lighter? But if I were, I wouldn't be me. Still, I wish I could be lighter. I couldn't stop thinking about the fact that he's married. And that I know his wife.

Am I really that ethical? Or is it my fear of *appearing* unethical, as well as overeager, that keeps me back? But between unethical and overeager, there's a large difference. The overeager fear is the fear of rejection—in order to avoid that, I leave the pursuit up to the man, so that he's the one who must risk rejection. I don't have the courage to come right out and say what I want, or desire.

I had brought along a volume of Attila József's poems, and on the way back from Gorlice to Budapest we did a line-by-line commentary, a veritable *explication de texte*, of a poem whose title caught my eye: "Gyáva vagy szeretni," "You are afraid to love." Did I think it referred to Gábor, or to me? "You have the most wonderful, varied ideas," he said when I suggested we read the poem. "It's impossible to sleep next to you."

Impossible to sleep next to you: the title of a hit song a few years back, he explained. Impossible to be bored, it meant. The thought popped into my head: "I wish you had slept next to me!" But I said nothing.

Yesterday morning, back in Budapest, I called Gábor at his office: "You left your umbrella in the car."

"I thought I might forget something."

In the evening, he called before coming over: "I'm flying." We spent a lovely half hour together. Then he was running down the stairs and I was calling after him: "On the road of life, we traveled two beautiful days together. God bless." Right after I said that, I felt like a fool. He would think me sentimental!

In the meantime, András came over this morning and was a great comfort and help. He went with me to the freight office to see about filling out the proper papers for shipping my trunk, then stayed near me at the airport until I passed through passport control and he couldn't see me anymore.

I am twice richer in affection and friendship, if not in love, as a result of my six months in Budapest.

FRIDAY, JULY 30—*Princeton, New Jersey*

This will be the story of my trip to Gorlice, the city of my father's birth. With a short detour in Cracow.

The Jewish quarter of Cracow on Monday morning—sunny, poor, almost deserted. An occasional tourist takes photographs of an old synagogue, now used as a carpenter's workshop, or an old religious school, cheder, its Hebrew inscriptions still on the wall celebrating the life of the study of Torah. But no children are there now. An occasional Pole looks at the tourists with boredom and wonder, and I imagine even some resentment: What's there to photograph in this slum? Can't the Jews leave well enough alone even now?

We walk around, following the addresses given in the guidebook, camera in hand. The Renaissance High Synagogue, now a museum of the history of Cracow Jews, stands on one side of a square with several boarded-up buildings; long ago the square must have been beautiful, for its proportions are noble. The synagogue is of reddish brick, massive, and looks restored. To our irritation the museum, which the guidebook said was open on Mondays, is closed. A poster advertising an exhibition on the Jews of Galicia stares at us, provocative, from a glass case on the wall.

Frustrated, we seek out the Remuh synagogue, also dating from the Renaissance—it's the only functioning synagogue in the city and is famous for its cemetery, where the last grave was dug in 1799. We find it tucked away on a street a few hundred yards from the High Synagogue. The building is small, and the prayer area feels tiny to me. The altar, the *bimah*, is enclosed in a wrought iron cage, and there are brass chandeliers hanging from the high ceiling. Otherwise the room is bare, whitewashed, with wooden pews. The women's section is slightly raised, behind a curtain. The stooped, elderly man who shows us around speaks German or broken English. He doesn't realize I'm Jewish and begins to explain things to which I have to say "I know, I know." He finally asks me, "Are you Jewish?" and seems happy when I say yes. "But he's not, right?" he says, pointing to Gábor. "Right." There are 150 Jews living in Cracow now, all of them old. To get the required ten men for a minyan is not easy—some people have to be paid to come. There's no rabbi, but there's a cantor. All of Poland has only one rabbi, and he lives in Warsaw. Before the war the Jewish population of Cracow was about 55,000.

Outside, we enter the large cemetery, surrounded by a brick wall we had seen earlier from the street. One whole length of the inner wall is a wailing wall, composed of broken bits of tombstones from the Jewish cemetery of a neighboring town, which the Nazis destroyed: they used the broken tombstones as paving stones. After the war, the Polish government paid to have the wailing wall built out of the fragments. Some are quite large—on one a pair of beautifully sculpted Torah scrolls stand out in relief. On all, bits of Hebrew lettering are visible. We take pictures.

"There are no shoemakers or carpenters buried here, only great wise men and students of the Talmud," our guide tells us, pointing to the tombstones. This guide is no longer the old man who spoke to us inside but the cantor himself—no spring chicken either, though a somewhat more sturdy figure. He is very proud of the elite status of these graves. This cemetery was safeguarded during the war by a ruse: the tombstones were taken down and laid flat, then covered with earth. "The Nazis knew there was a cemetery here, but they didn't want to take the time to unearth it. They were more interested in getting all the living Jews," the cantor explains. Good old Central European humor, András would say. The inside of the synagogue was spared because the Nazis used the space to store uniforms.

In the cemetery, a few people are busy among the tombstones. "Restoration work," the cantor says proudly. Gábor tells me the work is being done badly: the stones are scrubbed clean, but no attempt is made to restore any of the missing inscriptions. "They should photograph the stone as is, then get someone who knows Hebrew to try and reconstruct the missing texts based on what's there," Gábor explains. I toy with the idea of saying something to the cantor but quickly give it up. What's the use of making him feel bad? Besides, all of this is too sad.

Enormous Changes

After giving a donation, we walk out of the courtyard whose walls bear memorial tablets to victims killed by the Nazis. On the street, the sun is burning hot. A few children play in a nearby square, a young man hurries along the sidewalk in front of us. "You look depressed," Gábor says and offers me his arm.

Yes, I am depressed. Depressed at the indifference and the ruin, depressed at the disappearance of so many and the absence of their traces. Only empty shells remain. I can make notes, take pictures—futile gestures and at the same time necessary. We seek out two more synagogues. Gábor photographs them and also captures in the cemetery wall an empty window frame through which a green branch growing on the other side points a few leaves.

On the way to Gorlice, we were worried about time. The city hall, as far as we knew, closed at 3:00. What if we arrived a few minutes late and found the building and the offices closed? Gábor drove like a fiend ("I like this," he crowed as we zoomed along), but the two-lane highway in the midst of mountains imposed some restrictions. We barely had time to notice the magnificent scenery, which became truly spectacular after we reached Nowy Sącz. "We'll stop and admire on the way back. Now, full speed ahead." We reached the outskirts of Gorlice a few minutes before 3:00 and stopped the first man we saw. "Urzad miasta?" I inquired, reading from the sheet where I had written down the words for "city hall" in Polish. He looked puzzled, so I showed him the paper. "Oh—urzad miasta!" he said. He showed us the way in sign language. We thanked him and rushed on.

We parked the car and ran to the building. Wrong entrance. We ran around to the front, leaned on the door—it was 3:02, and for a wild moment I thought the door was locked. But it yielded, and we went inside. At the information desk I took out my paper again and pointed to the name of Pani (Mrs.) Spotowica. "Upstairs," the man said. We ran up the stairs and stepped into an open office.

"Pani Spotowica?" I asked. The young woman told us to follow her, and we went through a door marked "Sekretariat" into a small waiting room. There we were met by a plump, cheerful-looking, middle-aged lady with short dark brown hair, who, when she smiled, revealed a big silver front tooth. "Budapest?" she asked.

"Yes. We've come from Budapest." She took us into her office, crossing another one in which two young women looked at us curiously. I took out the letter Stani had written to Pani Spotowica, in flowery Polish, asking her to help us as much as possible in finding traces of the Rubin and Bressman families. After that we attempted to communicate in German and French; she knew neither of them well but had a bit of basic vocabulary in both.

The short answer was, the city hall had no documents relating to the Jews of Gorlice. The Nazis had destroyed all the Jewish records: birth and death certificates, marriage certificates, everything. My desire to obtain Daddy's birth certificate could not be satisfied.

Gábor and I looked at each other and looked at her. Come all this way for nothing? For a moment, no one could think of anything to say. "Are there any Jews living in Gorlice now?" I managed to ask her.

"No."

What about the neighborhoods where Jews had lived? Could she point them out to us?

At that moment, a somewhat younger man came into her office and they spoke rapidly in Polish. She dialed a telephone number and handed me the phone. At the other end, a woman's voice, speaking German: "Pani Spotowica doesn't speak German or French well enough. She asked me to talk to you." But what was there for me to ask? I sim-

ply repeated the question about Jews and the Jewish neighborhood. Were there any Jews living in Gorlice now? No,
there were none living there, but two gentlemen were in
town or had been temporarily. Where could they be
reached? I asked. I gave the phone back to Pani Spotowica,
who consulted her male colleague again in Polish. Before I
knew it, I was in the front room talking on the phone to
Mr. Risenberg. "Where are you?" he asked. We were
speaking in halting German (mine was halting, his was
OK). I told him, and he said: "You must come so we can
meet. I'm not far." He gave me the address, and I consulted
Pani Spotowica, who explained how to get there: just cross
the Rynek, the square, and follow the street down another
block.

Gábor and I left, thanking Pani Spotowica and her colleague with flourishes.

"He told me he now lives in Australia," I told Gábor as
we hurried through the square.

"In that case he must speak English," Gábor said. Sure
enough, a few minutes later we were being hailed, in English, by a small, sturdy white-haired man wearing a blue-
and-white sweater: "I've been waiting for you."

He escorted us into the house and introduced us to a
smiling Polish woman with deep-set eyes and a young man
he presented as her son. "These are the people I'm staying
with." Pani Boczon, wearing her ample kitchen apron,
ushered us into the dining room and asked whether we
would like coffee or liqueur. We gratefully asked for coffee,
thinking of the drive ahead. Her husband, a jovial round-
faced man with horn-rimmed glasses, joined us, and Mr.
Risenberg explained that Pan Boczon was writing a history
of the Jews of Gorlice.

Pan Boczon had consulted many archives. For example,
he had photocopied the voting list for 1928. He pulled out
the sheaf of pages and ran his finger down the *B*s. "Bress-

man—here they are." Six names were listed: Adela, born in 1904 and residing on Narutowicza Street, who was a hat-maker; Wolff, a shopkeeper born in 1892 and his wife Chaya, born in 1899, who lived on Ogrodowa Street; Pinkas, born in 1898, who was listed as *ohne Beruf* (without profession) and lived on Kosciuszski in the Zowodje district, slightly out of town; and Hinda and Sprinca, who were Bressmanowa—Bressman women—born in 1910 and 1903 and also residing on Kosciuszski in Zowodje. They must have been Pinkas's sisters, or perhaps Sprinca was his wife.

Were these Bressmans part of Daddy's mother's family? The birth dates suggest that Wolff and Pinkas could have been her younger brothers (she was born in 1884). Maybe they're the ones in the photograph I have of Daddy, stand-ing on a riverbank near Gorlice in 1936, ready to take a swim: he has on a bathing suit and looks as if he's about to jump into the water, while two fully clothed men wearing overalls look on. Daddy must have been on his own nos-talgia trip, visiting his birthplace where he had never lived. The place and date are written on the back of the photo-graph in his handwriting.

"I went to school with a Bressman boy," Mr. Risenberg tells me. "A fat kid; we used to tease him about it, the way kids do. He came from a very religious family, wore *payes*. I was from a much less religious family myself." Pan Boc-zon has now brought in a large book full of photographs, and Mr. Risenberg hands it to me: *Gorlice Book: The Com-munity at Rise and Fall*, ed. M. M. Bar-On (Israel, 1962). "This was published by the survivors of Gorlice," he tells me. It's in Yiddish; I can't read it, but the photographs are wonderful, showing the full range of life in the Jewish community before the war: study groups and music en-sembles, Zionist groups and gymnasium classes. The peo-ple range from stiff, white-shirted young men in buttoned-up suits and girls in prim blouses, their hair pulled back, who look like any other turn-of-the-century bourgeois youth, to bearded Chasidim in black hats and Talmud classes of young boys wearing yarmulkes, their fringed *tsitses* hanging out of their short pants. On page 121, in a school photo, Mr. Risenberg points to a young boy: "There, I think that was the Bressman boy." He looks like all the others, a boy of about eight or nine posing with his class.

In the meantime Pani Boczon has brought us coffee and cakes—two kinds of cakes, served on good china. And her husband has taken out all the materials he had gathered for an exhibition on the history of Jews in Gorlice, which was up at the museum for several months but is now closed. More photographs (a whole page of rabbis and "Talmudystas," including the last rabbi of Gorlice, white-bearded Elisha Halberstam), as well as a number of business letterheads and bills showing names and addresses of Jewish firms. Gábor, using my camera so that I will have the pictures, photographs the photos and the letterheads: Chaim Szymon Parnes, Salamon Wild, Emil Pister, Jakob Schwimmer—Where are they now?

Pan Boczon, Mr. Risenberg tells us, helped Jews during the war. He was in the Resistance and was taken to a concentration camp by the Germans. His name is pronounced like the French "Botchogne," he has told me in halting English, writing down the French version with special care. After that, I can see he's delighted whenever I call him by name, pronouncing it *à la française*.

Pani Boczon urges us to eat more cake. Mr. Risenberg tells us, "Her father and two brothers were killed by the Nazis for helping Jews." He translates for her what he has just said, and she nods her head. Extraordinary Poles, Pan and Pani Boczon! Pan Boczon, we learn, is a retired economist who has been commissioned by the city council to write histories of Gorlice. He gives me his two previous books, one of which is devoted to Gorlice during the war. On one page he points to a photo of three men, one middle-aged, two young: Pani Boczon's father and two brothers.

"I used to go to school with Jewish children, sit on the same benches," Pan Boczon says, smiling sadly. Yes, life was good before the war. "Jews here did very well—they got along with the Christians, there was never any trouble," says Mr. Risenberg. Before the war the population of the city was 8,000, half of them Jews. Today the population is 80,000; no Jews. Mr. Risenberg happens to be here because he's in the process of reclaiming his family's house on the Rynek, the main square in front of city hall. Pan Boczon is helping him fill out the necessary papers, go through the required bureaucratic steps. I don't suppose he'd ever move back to Gorlice, but he wants his house back for the principle of it. He has a daughter, born in Australia, who's now employed by one of the Australian consulates and is working in Frankfurt. Small world.

Mr. Risenberg escaped from Gorlice when the Germans marched in in 1939 (he was seventeen years old), fleeing to Lvov, which was in Russian hands. He was soon captured by the Russians and sent to a camp, but he survived and returned to Gorlice in 1945. Not long after that he left Poland for good. Now he divides his time between Australia and Israel, where he has many friends. In Australia, he owns beachfront real estate. "You have to live," he says.

By now it was 5:00, very late if we wanted to be back in Budapest before dawn. We all exchanged addresses and promised to write. Pan Boczon promised to keep his eyes out for Bressmans and Rubins as he continues his research. Gábor and I hugged Pan and Pani Boczon and left with Mr. Risenberg, who wanted to show us the house on the Rynek where he was born. There it was, near the corner, with four windows across. The fat Bressman kid had lived a few doors down, at number 12. Gábor took a photo of Mr. Risenberg and me in the doorway.

Now we really had to go. I had time only to run into the flower shop on the corner and buy a large bouquet for Pani Boczon. I gave it to Mr. Risenberg to take back to her, with my thanks, then hugged him good-bye. We sprinted back to the car, where we had left it hours earlier.

"It's extraordinary; you look completely revived—reborn!" Gábor said to me as we ran. Yes, strangely, after this exhausting afternoon I did feel revived, the exact opposite of the way I had felt when we left Cracow. Why? Why feel happy, in this city where not a single Jew was still living, where even the paper traces of the Jews had been so thoroughly obliterated that my father, as far as documents were concerned, had never been born? Was it because I had met a living Jew after all, who had walked these streets as a young man and remembered his youth as beautiful? Was it because I had met two extraordinary Poles who had helped Jews at their own expense and were continuing to help them? Or was it simply because I had carried out my once vague plan, visited the city of my father's birth and found some small trace of his family? (The man who kept the birth records for the Jewish Community was named Rubin. He too escaped into Lvov at the beginning of the war, taking his registers with him. But he was killed a few years later, and the records perished with him.)

Whatever it was, I felt good. We drove back through the high mountains as the sun was setting, lighting the horizon in pale reds and pinks and etching the far-off peaks in deep purplish blue.

By the time we reached Budapest, it was almost 2:00 A.M.

1994: ACACIA STREET

The traveler sets her watch to local time before locking her seat in an upright position and closing her tray table. She puts away her book and notebook, checks the pocket of the seat in front for stray items she might have forgotten, then settles back for the landing. After the plane has come to a complete stop, she undoes her seat belt and reaches in the overhead compartment for her jacket and carry-on bag—the word "Toshiba" is visible on the flap. She slips on the jacket, checks her briefcase one last time, smiles briefly at the woman next to her, then slings the computer bag over her shoulder and, carrying her briefcase, follows the other passengers off the plane.

Nobody is waiting for her, but she knows what to do. An hour later, the shuttle taxi deposits her in front of a gray building on a street just below the Vienna Gate entrance to Castle Hill. On the car radio, they're getting ready to announce the election results of the second round.

I'm back in Budapest for ten days, living in an apartment near the Collegium. The rector and all the staff have greeted me like a friend returning from a long trip. The rector has introduced me to this year's fellows and found me an office to work in. He's very proud of the institution's smooth functioning, and I congratulate him on it. He laughs his infectious laugh: "Well, it's thanks to you and the other pioneer fellows that we learned what to do!"

I've had joyous reunions with Eva and her husband, Aniko and Peter, András, Gábor. Eva recently finished the dissertation she had been working on for many years; Aniko has finished a translation and is leaving soon for a month in the United States; Peter's career is flourishing; András is as rotund as ever but owns two new suits that make him look elegantly portly; Gábor is as handsome and charming as ever, and as forbidden.

Everything feels familiar. I know which newspapers to buy, which movie theaters show old films, which plays must be seen, which bus to take to the Gellért. Mari is still there in the baths and gave me a superb welcoming massage to take away a year's aches and pains. András has resumed his role as guide, taking me to visit the park of discarded Communist statues that opened last August. Gábor and I, traveling again, took the cog railway up to my old mountain haunt "Normafa" and hiked all Sunday afternoon.

Why am I here? To add a new layer of nostalgia to the old one, now that 1993 has become another past to be revisited? To continue pursuing the childhood past, not yet over and done with? Or is nostalgia itself the thing I wish to leave behind?

Visiting the park of Communist statues is even more interesting now that the Socialists, who used to be Communists, have won the election. András and I have been discussing the results, like everybody else in Budapest. We're thrilled by the defeat of István Csurka's "Hungarian Truth and Life" Party, which failed to obtain a single seat in Parliament; Csurka himself won't be returning to Parliament, though he'll no doubt continue to write weekly columns for *Magyar Forum,* his right-wing newspaper.

The Socialists have invited the Free Democrats, who received the next largest share of the vote, to participate in a coalition. The invitation is a gesture of friendship (the Socialists don't need the extra votes; they have an absolute majority), and it looks as if the Free Democrats will accept. "It's a risk," says András, "since they'll be the junior partners and some unpopular economic measures lie ahead. Strictly speaking, they'd probably be better off staying outside the government and letting the Socialists take all the blame—but this way is more responsible." He voted for the Free Democrats.

"Do you think the Socialists will put the statues back?" I ask András jokingly as we walk toward the entrance of the park. Before 1989 these statues occupied places of honor all over the city; now they're displayed in a no-man's-land—a large, flat field from which the most striking view is of telephone poles and electric wires, on the outskirts of a village about twenty miles from Budapest. We took an intercity bus to get here. There's not exactly a crowd rushing to visit the park; besides the two of us, a family of English tourists are the only ones who got off at this stop.

"No, they won't put them back," András muses. "The past is dead. Well, not really dead—put in its place."

The entrance to the park is flanked by two huge statues: a full-length figure of Lenin and a double portrait, also full length, of Marx and Engels. "Guardians of the tomb," says András. "Lenin replaced Papa Stalin near City Park after the students pulled down his statue in 1956."

András remembers where most of the monuments used to be and tells me jokes about some of them. We've been given a small red sheet at the door, listing all the statues along with the name of the sculptor and the former place of each. There are forty-two statues here, ranging from small individual busts to colossal full figures. Among the colossal ones is the Soviet soldier who used to be on top of Mount Gellért, part of the monument celebrating the liberation of the city in 1945. I stand next to the soldier to be photographed: my head comes just above the hem of his long coat, slightly above his knee.

I'm surprised by how many monuments refer to the short-lived Kun regime of 1919. My favorite statue, a huge running figure waving a banner, very dynamic, represents a worker during the 1919 revolution. ("We used to say he was running after his girlfriend yelling, 'You forgot your panties, Gizi!'" András tells me, giggling.) It's as if the Communists after the war had needed to establish their own prehistory, their own heroes—like new artistic movements, which usually create their own set of artistic ancestors. After 1989 the same process occurred, but with different ancestors: one of the first gestures of the nationalist government was to put the crown of Saint Stephen back on the Hungarian shield.

"Are you worried about the Socialists' having won?" I ask András, returning to our previous topic as we walk around the grass.

"Not in the way you mean. I told you, there's no going back. What worries me is whether they'll manage to turn the economy around. Because if they fail we'll see the nationalists bouncing right back, and strong this time." He points to the colossal Russian soldier: "You see, ideology is not what interests people, whether Communist or nationalist. What they care about is the quality of their lives. They voted for the Socialists in the hope they would make things better. If they fail, the anger will be tremendous—and you know who always gets to play scapegoat when people become really frustrated and angry. We've seen it before, we may well see it again."

As usual, András looks on the dark side. The question for me is, What do we remember, individually and collectively, and what do we do with what we remember? What *should* we remember, and how? The park of discarded statues is an attempt to maintain the memory of the past but not to let it touch people's daily lives: get the statues out of the city. That's better than trying to eradicate the past altogether—by destroying the statues, for example, pretending they never existed. Wouldn't it have been even better to leave the statues in place, allowing the flow of history to wash over them like waves over pebbles on a beach?

Sounds good. But would I say the same about monuments to Hitler or Mussolini? Maybe some things are better off discarded, declared beyond the pale. Unfortunately, it's not enough to get rid of monuments in order to get rid of the prejudices in people's heads.

On one of my last days in Budapest, I take a trip to the Motherbook Office of the thirteenth district and obtain my birth certificate. András tracked down the proper district for me after I left last year—I was born in the Jewish hospital, not far from Margit Bridge. The notation in the ledger at the Orthodox Community Bureau, which listed a different clinic, was simply wrong. Now I possess three identical-looking documents, each one with its official stamp and serial number. When I return to the apartment, I spread them out before me: Mother's birth certificate, Mother and Daddy's marriage certificate (the one I got last year, not the older one), my birth certificate. They are all on pale blue paper folded in two, slightly bigger than a passport. These certificates are typed, not handwritten in spidery writing with a pen dipped in an inkwell. They are poor in information: no mention of religion, address, or anything else to flesh out the bones. The only remnant of poetry in them is the title on the cover, printed in block letters: ANYAKÖNYVI KIVONAT. Excerpt from the Motherbook.

Why has it meant so much to me to track down these pieces of paper? I cannot say, exactly. I experience deep pleasure in lining up the three "excerpts," unfolding them and placing them one on top of the other. They tell a story, however minimal: A girl is born, marries, and gives birth to a girl. The continuity of generations has prevailed over war and destruction, and I am the beneficiary of that victory.

A few months ago I reread a book I hadn't seen for over forty years, a classic French children's novel, Hector

Malot's *Sans famille*. It's a late nineteenth-century tale, an immediate best-seller when it was published, beloved by children ever since. I must have read it in Port-au-Prince in 1950, during the months we spent there waiting for a visa to the United States. We had lived for close to a year in Vienna, where my parents had put me in a French school. They didn't think it was essential I learn German. Now they put me in a school run by French nuns, the Sisters of Sainte Rose de Lima. My teachers were gentle and loving and almost succeeded in converting me. They gave me colored pictures of the Virgin Mary and a Saint Christopher medal when we left Haiti. It wasn't until we had spent several weeks in New York that I finally threw the medal out the window of our apartment. No, I wasn't a Catholic!

I already knew some French from Vienna, but it was in Port-au-Prince that I really started to read: the *Iliad* in a children's version, the moral tales of the Comtesse de Ségur (little girls who disobey their mothers fall into ponds or get chased by geese; good little girls get cakes and warm, fresh milk), and the book about the boy without a family, which I loved most of all. "I am a foundling. But until I was eight years old I believed that, like all the other children, I had a mother; for when I cried, there was a woman who held me so gently in her arms, cradling me, that my tears stopped flowing." That's how the story begins. At age eight little Remi is torn from the gentle peasant woman he calls Mother and from the only home he has known, a poor farmhouse on the outskirts of a village. He is sold by the woman's scheming husband (who was conveniently absent, working in Paris, for several years) to an old Italian singer who travels on foot throughout France with his trained dogs and monkey, giving performances in towns and villages on market days. Luckily for Remi, his new master is a kind man. He outfits him with city clothes and buys him real shoes instead of wooden clogs. He teaches him to sing and play the harp, to perform in little pantomimes with the animals, and to read. In the end, after many adventures and hardships, Remi discovers his real family, a family of English gentry, complete with manor house and a long line of ancestors. His only heartache is that old Vitalis, who was so good to him, did not survive to see him in his fortunate state.

One thing I had completely forgotten, but that seemed significant in retrospect: Malot dedicated the book to his daughter. The flowery paragraph of dedication, headed "To Lucie Malot," occupies a whole page. In identifying so strongly with the homeless hero, was I also playing the role of loving daughter to a great man? The adulation I felt for my father about that time seems to confirm that view.

When did I stop loving my mother? I cannot remember exactly. It was a gradual process, an accumulation of small changes, like a revolution. For years nothing seems to happen; then one day the world turns upside down.

I remember a film we saw in Vienna, a Hollywood life of Chopin. One scene toward the beginning shows Frederic leaving Poland, young and darkly handsome, already a great pianist. It's nighttime, he's dressed in his travel cloak, they're loading his baggage into a coach. A cloaked figure, mother or sister or best friend, embraces him tearfully. Before stepping into the carriage, Frederic stoops and picks up a handful of Polish earth. And another scene, toward the end: Frederic is in Paris, feted and loved and very sick. He's back from Italy, where he went with a bossy woman, George Sand. He gives a concert, playing his own pieces. Suddenly he starts coughing, and the ivory keys of the piano turn red.

For weeks after seeing that film, I went to sleep every night thinking about Chopin, who would forever have the face of Cornel Wilde. He was an artist, beautiful, doomed, far from home, and George Sand didn't understand him. I understood him, though; maybe I could have saved him. I was an exile too. Was I an artist too? I never asked. Art was a handsome young male, sensitive and dying.

Freud says a girl stops loving her mother when she realizes her mother lacks a penis—a crude way of saying that she becomes aware her mother lacks power. So she turns her love toward her father, whom she perceives as powerful and whose child she longs to bear. A family romance, "Vienna 1900" style. Freud doesn't imagine the little girl as wanting to be *like* her father, but I think I had both of those desires: I wanted to be like my father because he was a young male, and I was in love with him for the same reason. Obviously I wasn't aware of these thoughts at the time. But I knew I didn't want to be like my mother, an excitable woman who sometimes fell sick and had to be rushed to the hospital.

What I didn't know was that those sudden illnesses were miscarriages. After she lost the baby boy, she and my father both became obsessed with the desire to have another, a male child who would continue the family name. Twice in Budapest she started to bleed a few weeks into the pregnancy, and it happened again in Vienna. She spent several weeks in the hospital, her face pale and beautiful, afraid of death and complaining about the nurses.

I was happy to have my father to myself then. He was handsome and wore a mustache. His face crinkled when he smiled, all the way up to his eyes. His hands were finely shaped, the nails trimmed into neat ovals. One evening after visiting my mother in the hospital, we decided to walk home, crossing the square near Saint Stephen's Church. It was early March, still cold and windy, but the days were getting longer and people seemed in less of a hurry. We stopped for a moment to look at the church, slowly being restored from its bombings.

The twin towers were surrounded by scaffolding, bandages of wood. They looked dark, dramatic, like wounded soldiers. I held my father's hand and felt secure, almost conspiratorial. Around us people passed, chattering. I looked up at him, squeezing his hand. He smiled. Then I asked him whether he thought I was pretty. He hesitated for a moment, then said, "Of course." He quickly added: "Looks aren't everything. Brains are more important, even in a girl."

I was very smart, everybody said so. Why then, I wondered, did I have to fight back the tears?

I think of Mozart's operas, that fragile, beautiful world where everything ends well, but not before you think your heart will burst. Where have all the beautiful moments gone? the Countess cries in *Figaro*. Why is love followed by betrayal? In *Così fan tutte* it's the women who are fickle, "they all do it." But he should have said *tutti,* men included.

My father did it—at least I think he did—during the months we spent in Vienna. She was the mother of a friend of mine, a pretty blond girl with long braids. The mother was blond too. They were Hungarian refugees, marking time like us. We often went for walks with them on Sundays, and some nights the grown-ups went to the opera. I hated those nights because I had to stay home alone. I would leave the light on and go to sleep in my parents' bed. When they came home, they would transfer me to my room without waking me.

One night I woke up with the light still on. It was 2:00, no sign of my parents. I lay under the blanket, my body stiff, my mind numb: something had happened to them; they would never come back. When they arrived a half hour later, they found me sitting up in bed, eyes wide open. They hugged me, explaining they had gone out after the performance. I shouldn't have fretted so. Didn't I know they would never leave me? No, I didn't know. It still happens that if a friend is late to an appointment, I begin to imagine she has forgotten, or he has changed his mind.

When my mother went into the hospital, we began to see a lot of the blond girl and her mother. I would play at my friend's house after school, and sometimes when my father came to get me we stayed for dinner. Everybody laughed a lot, and I was sorry when it was time to go home. Some days my father came early and had tea in another room while we played.

After my mother came home from the hospital, those visits stopped. One night I heard my parents quarreling in their room. No, it was my mother screaming: "That blond whore! That blond whore!" The next day I heard her shouting on the telephone and guessed my friend's mother was at the other end. We never saw those people after that. Years later, in Miami on a visit to my mother, I found a picture of my friend and me in a box of old photographs. Two little girls in winter coats and bonnets, carrying muffs of rabbit skin. Foreign looking. There was a group picture too, of an earlier scene, September or October 1949. A band of friends sit around a picnic table in the woods, bareheaded in the afternoon sun. My girlfriend and I are at one side, making faces at the camera. Her mother is next to my father, but she's not looking at him. She's smiling at the camera. My mother sits on the other side and is smiling too.

My mother didn't believe in digging up the past. "Bad times, forget about that," she would say in her heavy accent as I rummaged through old photographs. Very rarely, she would laugh and start to talk to me about Budapest, ice-skating in City Park, ballet lessons, children's matinees at the opera or the theater. "Do you remember Latabár, the comedian, how funny he was? And Hansel and Gretel, do you remember?"

Yes, I remembered.

Acacia Street

Toward the end of December 1950, we boarded a plane in Port-au-Prince bound for Miami. Besides my parents and me, there was a brand-new baby sister—Eve Judith, born prematurely two weeks earlier, who traveled in a basket, swathed from head to toe in surgical cotton. From the airport in Miami we took a taxi to the hospital, where she was placed in an incubator for close to a month. During that time we spoke to my grandmother and my uncles by telephone and made plans to join them in New York. By the time we arrived in New York, I was able to make out the stories in *Little Lulu* comics; six months later, I was deep in *The Jungle Book*.

This could be the story. This is the story: survival, adaptation, luck. And never—almost never—looking back. What this has cost me, I am only now beginning to tally: abandoned friendships, lost loves, walls built around a solitude so deep that even motherhood cannot fully breach it. To others my life may look like a glittering palace. To me it sometimes feels like a bombed-out house, with only the walls still standing.

Then I think of my father, and I tell myself the only unlucky one, the one who paid the heavy price, was he. I am now several years older than he was when he died of a second heart attack, almost exactly ten years after we left Budapest. We were living in Chicago then, and I was home from college for the summer. The Hebrew school where my father taught was closed for vacation. My mother couldn't stand the city heat; she and my father and little sister moved to a resort on Lake Michigan, where he led the Saturday morning services at the synagogue and received the use of a small cottage as payment. I joined them occasionally on weekends but usually wished I hadn't. I was unhappy that summer because I was fat and felt helpless about getting thinner. I spent many hours in the library, watching the sailboats on the lake, or sprawled on my bed eating crackers and reading *Ulysses*. My mother nagged me about boyfriends, getting married, losing weight. My father wanted me to go to medical school. I wanted to eat and read.

My father had monthly appointments with a heart specialist downtown, who charged him less than his other patients because he was an immigrant and a man of learning. On his visit in late July, the doctor told him his electrocardiogram did not look good; he should go into the hospital. But my father worried about life insurance. He had just taken out another policy for five thousand dollars, and he hadn't told them about his heart condition. He decided to go to the hospital in Toronto, where his sister, my aunt Rózsi, lived.

Did he figure he could die in Canada without our losing the five thousand dollars? Ten years earlier, when the doctors gave him up, he made my mother put a copy of the Talmud under his pillow and told her fiercely not to cry. This time he packed a small suitcase and put his papers in order.

I drove him to the airport—it was still Midway then. I asked why he didn't go to the hospital in Chicago. "It's better this way," he said. When he reached the plane, crossing a strip of airfield and climbing the steps, he turned around and waved to me. He wore a wide-brimmed summer hat so that I couldn't see his eyes, but his mouth was smiling. Then he went inside the plane and did not look back.

A few days later he called me from Toronto. His voice on the telephone sounded exhausted, each word a huge effort. I tried to imagine him in his hospital bed, his head on the pillow with the receiver cradled against his shoulder. For years afterward he appeared to me that way in dreams, always sounding as if he were dying.

He asked me to come to see him, but said first I should drive to the cottage and spend the weekend with my mother and sister.

"I'd like to fly to Toronto right away," I said.

"Your mother wants to see you. A few days won't matter," he replied. So I packed up the car and drove to the small town on Lake Michigan.

I reached the cottage on Friday afternoon. After the first warm greetings, my mother began the usual reproaches: I was too fat, read too much, didn't care about her. I maintained an ironic silence. Then she told me she had to go to Chicago on Monday and was counting on me to stay with my sister. That loosened my tongue, for I had planned to fly to Toronto on Monday. A scene ensued, with both of us mouthing our well-rehearsed lines.

I: "You're petty, meanspirited, will never understand me." She: "You're a monster of selfishness. If your father's in the hospital, it's because of you. He worries about you all the time, even on his sickbed."

I finally agreed to wait an extra day.

Monday morning, I drove her to the train station. The rest of the day I swam and picked wild blackberries with my sister. That night, after my mother came home, we succeeded in avoiding a fight and went to bed early. I was packed to leave the next morning.

In my sleep, I heard the telephone ring. It was my aunt from Toronto. "You should all come," she said. Her voice sounded calm, but the words came slowly, as if choked. She did not say at first that he was dead, only kept repeating we should all come.

"If we come right away, will we see him alive?" I asked.

She waited. Finally she said in a low voice: "No."

He had died earlier that night, alone in his room. They had called her from the hospital when they noticed it.

"We had no idea how seriously ill he was! He didn't tell

227

anyone, not even the doctors." She sounded at once reproachful and pleading, as if asking to be forgiven for not being there when he died. The funeral would be the next day, in accordance with Orthodox law.

I drove us all to Midway Airport. We stopped at a gas station to go to the bathroom, and my sister asked me if we would ever see our father again. We wouldn't see him, but we could think about him, I told her. She started to cry, and I felt angry at myself.

I felt especially angry at my mother. She had stopped me from seeing him; now it was too late. She sobbed all the way to the airport, while I watched her in hate and silence. I wanted to hit her.

Our plane landed in Toronto at noon. When my mother saw my aunt, she burst into loud wails. What would become of her and her daughters, especially the little one? I said nothing while my aunt spoke to her soothingly. She drove us to her house. My uncle was there, with some Hungarian friends who had known my father. My aunt and I got back in the car to go see about the funeral arrangements.

We drove to the place where my father's body was. He was laid out in a bare wooden coffin as prescribed by the Law, wrapped in a white robe of fine cotton with lace trim around the collar, the robe he wore to synagogue on the High Holidays. (Did we stop to pick it up in Chicago on the way to the airport? Or had he packed it in his suitcase?) His face looked beautiful, like that of a very young man. He was forty-nine years old. The skin was soft and smooth and bore no makeup. I looked at him until my aunt pulled me away, and for the first time I cried.

The funeral took place that afternoon. It was hot and sunny. We watched them lower the coffin into the ground. The rabbi chanted the required prayer. My mother cried hysterically. I wore a borrowed black dress that felt too tight across my breasts.

A year later, I graduated from college and my adult life began. I had forgotten much but had to forget more if I wanted to move ahead. Budapest, childhood, father, all entered the park of discarded memories. I even tried to forget my mother, reducing my contact with her to ritualized visits and conversations where no real communication occurred. It was only when she too was near death that I began to remember. Perhaps because I glimpsed then, for the first time, how closely my life had followed hers, or because I realized her disappearance would block forever the full recapturing of my own history. Her approaching death signaled my own mortality.

But remembrance too has its traps. After you remember, and record, it's time to move again—not toward new forgetfulness, but toward new experience.

On the plane taking her from Budapest to Paris, the traveler suddenly remembers that on this trip she made no special effort to revisit the house where she had lived as a child. She passed in front of it with a friend one evening on the way to dinner, and they went inside so that she could show him the oblong courtyard and wrought iron railings. But the house that evening was simply a point along the way, not her destination. The traveler asks herself, Should she ascribe a heavy symbolic meaning to that distinction? No, but perhaps a light one.

Acacia Street, you have become part of my life.

Acknowledgments

Without the six months I spent in Budapest in 1993, this book would not have been written; without the many friends I made there, this book would not be what it is. As a fellow of the Collegium Budapest Institute for Advanced Study, I enjoyed the freedom of action and scholarly comforts that made writing possible and pleasurable; I am grateful to the Collegium's rector, Professor Lajos Vékás, as well as to all the staff, for their warm welcome. Rarely can one say that a single encounter has changed one's life, but I have the sense that every person I met in Budapest during those few months contributed to the intensity of the emotions I experienced there.

Besides all those who are a part of this book, a number of people have influenced its current shape and texture. Mary Morris's comments on "A Brief Vacation" helped me to understand the difference between inert and living prose— for her writerly encouragement at an early stage of this work, my heartfelt thanks. Another early reader of that chapter, Dorrit Cohn, inspired me with her enthusiasm. John Jacob, director of the Photographic Resource Center in Boston, invited me to exhibit parts of the 1993 diary, with photos and documents, at the center in the fall of 1994; his designs for the exhibition showed me that it was possible to turn everyday objects into art—I thank him for his dedication and for his belief in this work. Mary Gluck and Gerry Shapiro made detailed comments on the whole manuscript, earning my admiration for their critical acumen as well as my gratitude; Miklós Vajda kindly took on the role of "fact-checker" about Hungarian history and literature, sparing me many errors; Anne Engel, Ed Hiller, and Judy Sprotzer read the manuscript in one or more versions and offered precious commentary.

Acknowledgments

As always, the search for a title took many weeks and conversations, enrolling friends, family, and acquaintances. I am grateful to Anthony Alofsin, Patricia Baudoin, Marjorie Garber, Carol Gilligan, Barbara Johnson, Larry Kritzman, Warren Motte, Julie Pavlon, Naomi Schor, Robert Seydel, the whole Sprotzer family, Daniel Suleiman, Michael Suleiman, and Lucie White and her friends at the 1996 Association of American Law Schools convention in San Antonio for the energy they contributed to the search.

To Sander Gilman, who has taken an interest in this work from its earliest fragments and has proved to be an ideal reader, my profound and friendly thanks.

The shades of my parents, Michael N. Rubin and Lillian Rubin Farkas, have hovered over much of the writing of this book. I wish they could have lived to read it.